$1.95 EACH—WESTERN TRAVEL BOOKS FROM WARD RITCHIE PRESS

Trips for the Day or Week-end

ALL BOOKS COMPLETE WITH MANY PHOTOGRAPHS AND MAPS

QUANTITY		TOTAL
☐	**EXPLORING CALIFORNIA BYWAYS, #1** From Kings Canyon to the Mexican Border	$_____
☐	**EXPLORING CALIFORNIA BYWAYS, #2** In and Around Los Angeles	$_____
☐	**EXPLORING CALIFORNIA BYWAYS, #3** Desert Country	$_____
☐	**EXPLORING CALIFORNIA BYWAYS, #4** Mountain Country	$_____
☐	**EXPLORING CALIFORNIA BYWAYS, #5** Historic Sites of California	$_____
☐	**A GUIDEBOOK TO THE LAKE TAHOE COUNTRY**	$_____
☐	**A GUIDEBOOK TO THE MOJAVE DESERT OF CALIFORNIA,** Including Death Valley, Joshua Tree National Monument, and the Antelope Valley	$_____
☐	**A GUIDEBOOK TO THE MOUNTAINS OF ORANGE AND SAN DIEGO COUNTIES**	$_____
☐	**A GUIDEBOOK TO THE NORTHERN CALIFORNIA COAST, VOL. I.** Highway 1	$_____
☐	**A GUIDEBOOK TO THE NORTHERN CALIFORNIA COAST, VOL. II.** Humboldt and Del Norte Counties	$_____

[SEE MORE BOOKS ON OTHER SIDE]

WARD RITCHIE PRESS
3044 Riverside Drive, Los Angeles, Calif. 90039

Please send me the Western Travel Books I have checked. I am enclosing $_____, (check or money order—no currency or C.O.D.'s). Please include the list price plus 25¢ a copy and 25¢ for each additional copy to cover mailing costs.

Name _____

Address _____

City _____ State _____ Zip Code

S0-EKK-921

A GUIDEBOOK TO THE
LAKE TAHOE COUNTRY
Volume I

With patience the Tahoe fisherman can land that coveted "big one."

GUIDEBOOK TO THE LAKE TAHOE COUNTRY

VOLUME I

Echo Summit, Squaw Valley and the California Shore

BY MIKE HAYDEN

EDITED BY RUSS LEADABRAND

WARD RITCHIE PRESS · LOS ANGELES

THIS BOOK IS
DEDICATED TO
OLGA

First Printing, September 1971

CONTENTS

*Early day logging in Lake Valley. Picture probably
taken in 1880s. Photo from collection at the
California State Library.*

I INTRODUCTION TO THE TAHOE AREA

"And I have not said a word of its water, which is so blue that it seems impossible that it should not stain, and so clear that one can see fishes swimming more than a hundred feet below his boat, and so cold that ice would not cool it."—BITS OF TRAVEL AT HOME by H. H., 1887.

Lake Tahoe for its size, depth, and beauty is one of the great alpine waters of the world. It ranks with Yosemite Valley as a showplace of the Sierra Nevada. Visitors have been extravagant in their praise of Tahoe's splendor since the first hotel on the lake opened its doors in 1860.

Tahoe, in the summer of 1861, impressed Mark Twain as "the fairest picture the whole earth affords."

While camped on the South Shore in 1870, Joseph Le Conte, a founder of the Sierra Club, logged in his journal, "Of all the places I have yet seen, this one I could enjoy the longest and love the most."

A century later, Tahoe is still beautiful and almost too popular. Indeed, so much attention is presently focused on the lake, a stranger might assume it to be the sole attraction of the Northern Sierra. Yet, if Tahoe were to vanish overnight, its blue expanse replaced by sagebrush flats, most of the territory covered in this guidebook would still be fraught with interest for the traveler who delights in spectacular mountain country.

For Tahoe lies at the hub of a fiercely romantic region on the Sierra Crest that is as fascinating for its history as for its charms

E. J. "Lucky" Baldwin's "Tallac House" was the most fashionable resort on Lake Tahoe in the Gay Nineties. Mount Tallac with its famous "cross of snow" may be seen through the trees on the right. From the collection at the California State Library.

as a mountain playground. The local lore is steeped in tall tales and colorful legends. Many of these hark back to the early mining excitement when Sierra passes in the Tahoe area bore the brunt of traffic to the diggings.

This book will trace the Emigrant Trails on which the Forty Niners trekked to the Mother Lode and the toll roads on which a fantastic movement of men, mules, and wagons streamed east to Nevada's Comstock Lode. Reference will be made to the years when Tahoe's water and timber were exploited to serve the mines. It was during this period the spectacle of logging and fluming drew tourists to Tahoe from places as far away as England and the Continent.

The sites of old mining centers in the Tahoe area will be listed. Few of these were productive except in Alpine County where deposits of gold, silver, copper, and sulphur were worked.

The book will list people as well as places that figured in the drama of early exploration and settlement. To mention a few, there was E. J. "Lucky" Baldwin, bon vivant and avid speculator, who parlayed a fortune in mining stock and spent part of it to build Tallac, "The Summer Resort of the World."

There was a postman on skis, John A. "Snowshoe" Thompson, who packed mail over the Sierra for twenty winters. There was Henry J. "Hank" Monk, a superb story teller and dashing "Knight of the Lash" whose stagecoach transported such notables as Horace Greeley and Rutherford B. Hayes. There was "Crazy Judah" who surveyed an "impossible" railroad and Charles Crocker who did more than anyone to make Judah's dream come true.

There was the lovely and indefatigable Mrs. Sierra Nevada Phillips Clark who pioneered a fashionable spa in rugged back country. And the gifted Washoe Indian woman, Louise Keyser, who fashioned baskets of extraordinary beauty. And the edu-

9

cated gentlewoman, Tamsen Donner, who stoically endured the horrors of starvation in a winter bivouac only to perish in a vain effort to save her family.

There were the mountain men, Kit Carson, who scouted for Fremont's second expedition, and the redoubtable Caleb Greenwood, who guided the first wagon train over the Sierra when he was 82 years of age.

Not to be upstaged was the Comstock magnate, "Slippery Jim" Fair. For a lark, he persuaded a tenderfoot New York reporter to join him on a terrifying boat ride down Mount Rose on the world's longest lumber flume.

There was the good Doctor Bourne who masterminded a campaign to change Tahoe's name to "Lake Sanatoria." And the notorious gunfighter, James Stewart, the "Silent Terror of the Sierra." And the celebrated J. V. Varney whose five-piece brass band played for champagne parties on the lake steamers. And the British gentleman of leisure, Sir Edward Dalles, who fished Tahoe on a June evening in 1881 and caught 1,000 pounds of trout with his illuminated "electric hook and line."

Most of the well-remembered names are Anglo-Saxon, but the people were of many national backgrounds. The given name of "Snowshoe" Thompson, a Norwegian by birth, was Jon Torsteinson Rui. Among the stalwarts on Fremont's second expedition was Jacob Dodsworth, a free black man. The mother of Caleb Greenwood's sons was of the Crow Nation. Michael Spooner, for whom Spooner Summit is named, was French-Canadian, as were many of the lumberjacks who logged the Tahoe Basin. Most commercial fishermen at the lake were of Portuguese or Italian descent. The difficult and dangerous work of building a railroad over Donner Pass was largely accomplished by 10,000 artisans from China.

The Tahoe Area may be spoken of to include the Feather River Country and also the western edge of the Great Basin that is occupied by Reno and Carson City. It was the feeling of the editor, Russ Leadabrand, and myself that these areas deserved coverage in separate volumes. So this book will concentrate on the Sierra Crest from Truckee Summit approximately 80 miles south to Ebbetts Pass and the headwaters of the East Carson River.

This country is subdivided by the rugged topography into three distinct regions—Alpine County, the Tahoe Basin, and the Donner-Truckee Area. Each is a world of its own with a different look and feel about it. Together they pose a startling paradox in terms of development.

For example, the largest settlement on the 450-mile crest of the Sierra is found on the south shore of Lake Tahoe. Here is a bustling, up-to-date city of 30,000 population, complete with traffic jams, urban sprawl, and high-rise buildings.

But just three miles west of city limits is the boundary of the 100-square-mile Desolation Wilderness. This is a rugged, lake-dotted highland where no vehicles are permitted and the only improvements are trails.

A slender "buffer zone" between the Desolation Wilderness and the City of South Lake Tahoe is the Tallac area of the El Dorado National Forest. Here are gentle, pine-scented nature paths and some of Tahoe's most inviting swimming beaches.

Accommodations in the Desolation Wilderness amount to primitive clearings with space to build a cookfire and stretch a sleeping bag.

The Tallac area has rustic resorts and improved roadside campgrounds.

South Lake Tahoe groans from the crush of 225 modern motels.

Enclaves of urban living are nothing new in the Tahoe area. In an earlier age, there was Glenbrook, a booming lumber center on Tahoe's east shore. The mills here cast an ugly pall of smoke

11

on the lake when the wind was right. Now the site is occupied by summer cottages and a handsome old inn.

South of Tahoe in Alpine County, there was Silver City. The site is marked by the ruins of an old jail.

Near Henness Pass in the Donner-Truckee area, there was the City of Meadow Lake. In 1866, this mining center boasted 500 homes, stores, and office buildings, many of them brick, and about 5,000 residents. Today, you must search diligently at Meadow Lake to find a clue that people ever lived here.

What remained after the early settlements faded were wagon roads. These were gradually reconstructed to provide the present system of scenic highways on which the car-explorer may sample every corner of the Tahoe Area.

There is still some logging and cattle grazing around Tahoe, but mining is almost a thing of the past. The local economy now depends on tourism and outdoor recreation. In summer, recreation is centered on the streams and several hundred lakes, most of which contain trout and lie inside the boundaries of the El Dorado, Tahoe, Toiyabe, or Stanislaus National Forests.

This guidebook will list such attractive roadside waters as Alpine, Caples, Donner, and Fallen Leaf Lakes which afford swimming, boating, and camping, as well as trout fishing. There will be mention of back country lakes, some remote, and some situated within an easy hour's walk of the nearest road.

The National Wilderness System is represented in the Tahoe Area by the Desolation area and the 50,000-acre Mokelumne Wilderness. The book will examine these and also a number of primitive areas in the National Forests, such as the Granite Chief area, which enjoy much the same protection as units in the official Wilderness System.

A portion of the Tahoe-Yosemite Trail will be covered. Only four roads are crossed by this exciting footpath on its 180-mile run from Meeks Bay to Tuolumne Meadows.

There's too much wilderness in the Tahoe Area for this guide to enumerate all the lakes and trails. However, a number of publications will be cited which provide this kind of information.

The only large population centers in the Tahoe Area are found at opposite ends of Lake Tahoe. Here the recreational potential includes such urban-oriented pursuits as golf and gambling, as well as every water-oriented sport except surfing.

The Tahoe Basin will be examined in the next chapter. Suffice to stress here that there's no off season at Tahoe. For one thing, it's estimated forty per cent of visitors come to gamble and this is a year-round, twenty-four-hour activity at the larger casinos.

The alpine winter lasts about six months. It may snow as early as October and some ski areas remain open through April. The Tahoe area holds the largest concentration of winter sports facilities in the West. In a normal year, South Lake Tahoe receives eighteen feet of snow and some areas of back country get more than thirty feet. This book will list the ski areas and also some gentle slopes which afford sledding and tobogganing. The possibilities for skating and snowmobiling will be covered.

Spring comes in May, but the weather stays fickle through June with a high quota of chill, wet, blustery days. Some high lakes may remain snowbound into July. However, the period from April through June affords the choicest fishing at Tahoe.

Summer is balmy and nearly rainless. On weekends and holidays, there is congestion everywhere on the lakeside. The beaches are blanketed with lazy sunbathers and frolicking children. Camps in the State Parks and National Forest recreation areas are filled. Motel vacancies are at a premium and the rates are high. Traffic is heavy, even on some foot trails in the Desolation Wilderness.

Autumn sets in shortly after Labor Day. Then the crowds fade, the aspens glow, and trout fishing peaks in the high lakes. Temperatures are apt to plummet below freezing

Two views of the steamer Tahoe *in Emerald Bay.*
Photos from collection at the California State Library.

after sundown but there are many beautiful Indian summer days when there is almost no breeze and Tahoe is flat calm. A brief resurgence of traffic occurs when the hunting season opens.

Of four major trans-Sierra highways which cross the Tahoe Area, only two remain open when the snow flies. State Highway 4, the "Big Trees Route" over Ebbetts Pass, and State 88, which spans Carson Pass, are usually closed by mid-December. The steep and winding Highway 4 is the least traveled route in summer. But it and the recently improved Highway 88 are widely regarded as two of the most scenic drives in North America. In years of heavy snowfall, neither road becomes passable at the summit until late June.

The heaviest traffic is borne by Interstate 80, a freeway which spans the Sierra Crest near the old Donner Pass. US Highway 50 over Echo Summit skirts Tahoe's southeast shore before it ascends the Carson Range by way of Spooner Summit. Portions of US 50 have been converted to freeway, but it's still a winding two-lane road where it approaches Tahoe on the historic Meyers Grade.

All the trans-Sierra roads, including the old Henness Pass route, are intersected near the crest by State Highway 89. This road enters the Tahoe Area at Truckee Summit and leaves to the south by way of Monitor Pass. It traces Tahoe's west shoreline and affords access to miles of productive trout water on the Truckee, Little Truckee, and Upper Truckee Rivers and on both forks of the Carson River.

Although classed as "all weather" roads, both US 50 and Interstate 80 are subject to temporary closures during storms. State 88 is expected to achieve "all weather" status by the winter of 1972-73. Portions of Highway 89 and most forest spurs and secondary roads covered in this guide remain snowbound through early spring.

Motorists are required to carry tire chains and a shovel is

recommended for winter travel anywhere in the Tahoe Area. Also it's a good idea to carry blankets in the event your car becomes stalled in a storm. Temperatures down to zero are common in December and January.

The roads, plus a few old buildings, flumes, and mine shafts, comprise the Tahoe Area's only visible links with its lively past. Gone are the early homesteads, inns, toll houses, fish landings, and Pony Express stations. Gone too are the logging railways and graceful lake steamers. Little remains standing of the health spas and palatial resorts which catered to the Comstockers. Only ruins and rusty artifacts memorialize the proud cities that mushroomed in the wilderness.

So much has gone, so much in the Tahoe Area is entirely new, and yet the rugged Sierra peaks loom the same for the motorist as they did for the covered wagon trains. In a brief informal way, this guide will try to recapture the excitement of the early years but always with an eye on the Tahoe Area today, which has its own charisma.

II INTRODUCTION TO THE TAHOE BASIN

"The final hard truth about Lake Tahoe, it seems to me, is that without tough federal action and the leadership to bring it about we will proceed to corrupt Tahoe beyond the economic and technical ability of this generation to redeem it."— LAKE TAHOE by Alfred Heller, 1965.

The impact of man on Tahoe hardly shows when the lake is viewed from a high promontory, such as Inspiration Point on Highway 89. Here, the traveler sees a vast expanse of open water, edged by dark forest and occasional white sand beaches, and completely ringed by imposing peaks and ridges.

Buildings, roads, and utilities are, for the most part, screened by the foliage. Only a few structures, such as the high-rise casinos, loom above the trees.

The scene has changed little since Colonel "Cockeye" Johnson trudged up from the Mother Lode to explore the shoreline in 1853. In that year and for decades afterward, Tahoe was a lake of mystery.

Tourists in the Sixties were warned not to go swimming in the lake. It was believed a person would sink instantly in Tahoe's crystalline snow water.

The notion that Tahoe was "bottomless" endured into the present century. How else to explain why the bodies of drowned persons were rarely recovered? But this mystery was solved when it was found the frigid temperatures in Tahoe's depths tend to preserve all organic material that enters the lake. Since there is no decomposition, no gases form that would float a body to the surface.

Despite many surveys, the first by Day and Goddard in 1855, the precise location of Tahoe with respect to the California-

Pierce Arrow stage at Rubicon Springs Hotel in 1919.
From the collection at the California State Library.

Nevada boundary was not determined until late in the previous century. This worked a hardship on some Tahoe residents who could not be certain from year to year to which state and county they were obliged to pay taxes.

Tahoe is the third deepest lake in North America. The average depth is 980 feet. Absolute bottom is 1,645 feet below the surface. The normal high water mark is 6,229 feet above sea level. The maximum storage of water approaches ten trillion gallons, which is enough to cover all of California and Nevada to a depth of several inches.

Tahoe stretches 21.6 miles long and up to 12.2 miles wide to encompass 193 square miles. These dimensions are not impressive compared with some low elevation lakes. But, allowing for the volume of water, Tahoe may be considered one of the largest alpine lakes in the world.

On a grey day, Tahoe looks grey. When the sun shines, the lake is brilliantly hued in multiple shades of green and blue. The vivid colors are attributed to the purity of the water. Out beyond the primary shelf the water may appear nearly black because of its great depth.

Tahoe is replenished by seventy feeder streams. Largest of these is the Upper Truckee River, which rises near Carson Pass. The only outlet is the Truckee River. The total area of the Tahoe Basin is 502 square miles.

Because of its depth, Tahoe never freezes over except at Emerald Bay.

Most of the Sierra's 1,500 lakes were excavated by glaciers late in the Pleistocene epoch. The shaping of Tahoe began earlier. It was part of the process which transformed the east slope of the Sierra from a moderate incline, similar to the west slope, into the steep, abrupt drop-off it is today.

Perhaps 750,000 years ago, the subterranean pressures which gave rise to the Sierra caused the earth's crust to crack in a number of places on the range. The cracks on the west slope were minor because here was a single block of granite many miles thick. But some cracks on the east slope developed into faults and, later, segments of crust between the faults sank to create such depressions as Death Valley and the Owens Valley.

In the case of Tahoe, two parallel faults developed near the summit of the Sierra. Later, a slippage between the faults resulted in a deep trench eighty miles long. It stretched from the vicinity of Echo Summit to Sierra Valley where the Feather River rises. The trench was flanked on the west by the main Sierra crest. On the east was a "splinter" of peaks and ridges today known as the Carson Range.

Tahoe was born when Mount Pluto rose from the trench to impound the present basin with a wall of lava rock. Over the ages, the lake rose and fell as the basin was modified by erosion, including glacial action, and by further eruptions of lava.

The modification of Tahoe by man started in the 1870's when a low dam was built at the outlet. Before then, the Washo and other Indians had hunted and fished in the basin for centuries without effect on the natural setting. The bulk of Forty-Niners had passed within a few miles of Tahoe, only dimly aware of its existence.

The few emigrants who saw Tahoe were those who followed a difficult trail blazed by "Cockeye" Johnson in the spring of 1848. This trail ran up the east slope of the Carson Range, contoured south along the crest, gradually descending to Lake Valley. From Lake Valley, the trail climbed a fierce grade known as Johnson's Hill to Echo Summit, which was formerly known as Johnson's Pass. From here, the trail dropped to Placerville along the approximate route of US Highway 50.

In 1851, Absalom Woodward and Major George Chorpening, "the father of the Pony Express," obtained a contract to pack mail from Sacramento to Salt Lake City by way of Echo Summit. This same year, Tahoe's first settler, Martin Smith, built a log cabin in Lake Valley and hung a sign outside the door which read, "Groceries—meals at all hours and lodgings if required."

Fred Bishop and "Daddy" Dritt carried mail over Echo Summit on skis in the winter of 1853-54. The following summer, Asa Hawley started work on a road to replace the steep trail up Johnson's Hill. At the same time, Seneca Marlette directed a survey of the first "grand trunk" road over the Sierra. The route selected followed "Johnson's Cut-off" from Placerville to Echo Summit and thence by way of Hawley's Grade south to Luther Pass and Hope Valley. From Hope Valley, the descent to Nevada was made on the Carson Emigrant Road, now known as Highway 88.

The new road was authorized by the California Wagon Road Act of 1855. But after the legislature failed to appropriate funds, several of the counties financed the work. As each section of road was completed, the franchise to collect tolls and maintain the right-of-way was assigned to a private company. The first stage coach crossed over Echo Summit in June of 1857.

In June of 1859, a rich strike was reported in the Comstock Lode, twenty miles east of Tahoe. Overnight, traffic jams developed on the "grand trunk" road which was single lane with turnouts. Inns and road houses sprang up and the toll houses raked in fortunes in fees.

And so, Johnson's Cut-off became the Great Bonanza Road to the Washoe. And Tahoe became an oasis for the supply trains, a source of hay, fish and game, and of vegetables that were cultivated on flats along the lakeshore.

Business boomed until the railroad over Donner Pass was completed to Reno in 1868. By then, two "dog legs" of the Bonanza Road were in use. These were the Kingsbury Grade Road over Daggett Pass and the Lake Bigler Toll Road which followed the present route of US Highway 50 around Tahoe's southeast shore to Glenbrook and Spooner Summit.

Bigler was the name given Tahoe following a visit by California's third governor, John Bigler, to Lake Valley in 1852. Before then, Tahoe was variously known as Mountain Lake, Big Truckee Lake, and Lake Bonpland. In 1861, Governor Downey tried to change the name to Tula Tulia. The Civil War had begun and John Bigler espoused the Confederate cause.

On a map published in 1862, the lake appeared as Tahoe. The change was made by William Knight, a Union sympathizer, at the suggestion of Dr. Henry De Groot who claimed Tahoe was a Washo word meaning "big water." The name stuck but in 1870 the California legislature made Bigler the official name. This was not revoked until 1945.

The railroad brought hard times to Lake Valley. But the Comstock still had need of Tahoe's timber. This was supplied by the mills at Glenbrook and Incline. Logging was a major enterprise in the Tahoe Basin until the mines gave out in the 1880's.

The cream of society in the Gay Nineties was seen at Tahoe playing croquet on the lawns of the Tallac House or sampling the mineral water at Brockway Hot Springs. Logged-over land near the shoreline was purchased for little more than back taxes and made into magnificent private estates or subdivided for summer cottages.

A delegation of farmers, equipped with shovels and dynamite, turned up at Tahoe City in 1903 to excavate a channel that would bypass the dam at the outlet. A pitched battle with Tahoe residents was narrowly averted. This was one of many bitter episodes in the struggle for Tahoe's water that began in the 1870's and continues up to the present day.

Tahoe was still fashionable in the 1920's when there was considerable automobile traffic to the lake. The last excursion steamer ceased to operate in 1934. The big bands of the Forties played at the elegant Tahoe Tavern which adjoined the first winter sports area on the lake. Shortly after Pearl Harbor, the Southern Pacific cancelled its "Snowball Specials" to Tahoe City.

Tahoe was a quiet place when the war ended with less than a thousand winter residents. There was only one casino on the South Shore, housed in a log structure near Bijou.

The present boom in recreation and real estate began in the early 1950's when improved roads, new ski bowls, and heavy promotion by developers and gaming interests drew throngs to the basin.

The sudden influx of visitors led to breakdowns of the sanitary treatment plants. There were instances of raw sewage spilling into the lake. Large amounts of silt were discharged by the tributary streams. This was blamed on bulldozers laying out streets and clearing sites for hundreds of new homes and service industries.

Spokesmen for the developers depreciated the pollution as "growing pains." But scientists such as UC Professor Charles R. Goldman warned the clarity of the lake was threatened.

Goldman, the foremost authority on the limnology of Tahoe, pointed out that both silt and sewage contain nutrients which contribute to the rapid aging of a lake. This process, known as eutrophication, involves a proliferation of green algae and other aquatic plant life. Goldman cited the possibility of an "algae bloom" whereby an ugly scum forms on the water which has a strong and disagreeable odor.

Many residents protested the rash of new construction which they feared would destroy the beauty of the lakeshore. But officials of the five counties which share Tahoe insisted they were competent to deal with all environmental problems and insure "orderly development."

Finally, in 1967, the threat of Federal intervention caused California and Nevada to set up the Tahoe Regional Planning Board, or TRPA. At first, this consisted of two agencies operating independently on opposite sides of the state line.

The California TRPA gave local government the dominant

An early-day photo of the Rubicon River at Rubicon Soda Springs. From the collection at the California State Library.

voice in decision-making. Even so, the counties of Placer and El Dorado withheld funds from the agency and instigated legal proceedings against it.

In two years, the California TRPA approved more than sixty subdivisions and suffered a lot of abuse. Lake dwellers charged it with failing to control development and curb such violations as the illegal cutting of trees. The subdividers and county officials complained it had placed the local economy in a "strait jacket."

The Nevada TRPA fared better but was criticised for its approval of high rise casinos.

In 1969, President Nixon and the Congress authorized creation of a bi-state Tahoe Regional Planning Agency and directed it to prepare a master plan for development. In the same year, the California Legislature passed the Porter-Cologne Water Quality Control Act. A provision in this act set a deadline of January 1, 1972, for the export of all sewage from Tahoe to locations outside the basin.

With the help of a computer, the staff of the new bi-state TRPA collated and digested thousands of facts about Tahoe. Most of the information came from studies by specialists from the universities and a score of government agencies.

In May of 1971, the TRPA released its Master Plan. The recommendations in this document drew an angry response from the developers.

As was stated earlier, Tahoe is still beautiful when viewed from a high place. But, to evaluate the Master Plan, we must examine the lakeshore at close range. A study team from UC Davis did this and found that only 41% of the vegetation around Tahoe remains in its natural state. About 40% of the lakeshore is bound by powerlines and 13% of the roads that would otherwise enjoy a scenic view of the lake are screened by buildings, billboards, and electric signs.

One effect of this urbanization is the crowding out of native wildlife. A Forest Service report lists thirteen endangered species at Tahoe, including the pileated woodpecker, golden eagle, and Washoe chipmunk.

The lake water is still "remarkably pure" according to the US Geological Survey which reports one pound of dissolved minerals in 1,800 gallons. However, the USGS cautions that the danger of eutrophication is very real. Green algae is visible in the shallows near built-up areas of the lakeshore. Siltation is still a cause for worry but the sewage problem is being solved.

Operating at South Lake Tahoe is one of the most advanced sanitary treatment plants in the world. Here effluent is processed into clear water that is safe to drink. This water is piped out of the basin instead of being returned to the lake only because it contains nitrates and phosphates which might contribute to eutrophication.

In summer, the basin is hung over with smog. Several forest lookouts were closed in 1970 because the haze was too thick for the fire watchers to spot a column of smoke. The smog is harmful to the trees, many of which have been weakened by disease, erosion, and land fills. Some die-off has been traced to the rock salt used to keep the roads clear of ice.

By latest count, the basin has 75,000 full- and part-time residents and a maximum population of 130,000 on summer weekends. This is a bit below the ceiling recommended by the Master Plan. There are 27,000 vacant lots in Tahoe subdivisions. A TRPA estimate based on present zoning projects a peak population of 750,000. With this many people, the Stanford Institute calculated Tahoe would require 40 to 60 freeway lanes on the North Shore and 80 to 100 lanes on the South Shore.

The legislation which established the TRPA posed this question—"To what degree can man intrude his normal pattern of use and development and still retain the very qualities of the environment which attracted him to the area?"

26

By way of reply, the Master Plan recommends against further development of the Tahoe Basin. It strongly implies that some areas already developed at Tahoe should be phased out and allowed to revert to their natural state.

In June 1971, the TRPA rejected the plan and ordered its staff to try again. It seems unlikely any plan can be adopted that is not acceptable to the developers.

Of course, Tahoe's predicament arises because people choose to live at the lake rather than be content to visit there, as in the case of the National Parks. Yosemite has its headaches, but it enjoys a much higher rate of tourism than Tahoe with minimal effect on its beauty.

An opportunity was lost in 1921 when some Tahoe residents lined up 75% of the land for sale to the federal government at $5 million. When the group approached the National Park Service, it was told to come back when it could speak for the other twenty-five per cent. So today, half the basin is National Forest but only sixteen miles of shoreline is public. The other 55 miles of frontage is private and posted. As of 1971, the going rate for frontage at Tahoe was a thousand dollars a running foot.

It may be too late for a National Park but the outlook is bright for some kind of federal preserve at Tahoe. Senator Alan Bible of Nevada has proposed a National Lakeshore and a year-long feasibility study was authorized by Congress in 1970. The state parks at Emerald Bay and the rapidly expanding Lake Tahoe Nevada State Park could provide huge blocks of unspoiled land for such a preserve.

Good roads approach Tahoe from many directions. In the next chapter, we will motor to the lake on Highway 50 because it seems appropriate to begin with the oldest, most historic route. Hopefully, this brief account of Tahoe's colorful past and controversial present will add to your enjoyment of the trip.

*Upper Lake Valley. California Highway 89 on the left
and Johnson's Hill on the lower right.*

III LAKE VALLEY

"When the teamsters stopped at night or noon, the road in front of the stations at which they halted would be blockaded for a great distance, and it looked almost as though all the teams in California were crossing the Sierra in one grand caravan."— THE BIG BONANZA by Dan DeQuille, 1876.

The drive from Sacramento to Lake Tahoe by way of Highway 50 is 100 miles. If you have an hour or so to spare, the capitol city is worth a stop to browse through the exhibits at Sutter's Fort State Historic Park at 2701 "L" Street. Here, in the adobe stronghold built by John Sutter in the 1840's, are many pioneer artifacts and such memorabilia as a doll cherished by Patty Reed of the Donner Party and a section of tree from Carson Pass on which Kit Carson carved his initials.

Placerville in the Mother Lode invites another stop for its old buildings and the quaint layout of its streets. This former mining center, which is 45 miles east of Sacramento, has associations with Lake Tahoe which date back to its founding in 1848. The town was first known as Dry Diggings and then, for a time, as "Hangtown" because of the hangings which followed a violent outbreak of crime. An excellent description of the Placerville area is found in the Sunset book, "Gold Rush Country."

At Riverton, a few miles inside the El Dorado Forest boundary, US Highway 50 enters the rugged South Fork Canyon of the American River. Here, the freeway ends and the highway begins more nearly to approximate the steep and winding course of the Great Bonanza Road to the Washoe. This road became California's first State Highway in 1896.

Trout Creek photographed off the Pioneer Trail Road.

Few traces are left of the roadhouses that sprang up on every flat along the route after Henry Tompkins Paige Comstock, otherwise known as "Old Pancake," struck pay dirt at the head of Gold Canyon. Many of the old Bonanza inn sites are signed by bronze historical markers and some are occupied by El Dorado Forest campgrounds.

Thirty-nine miles up the road from Placerville is the 39 Mile Camp. Here the north wall of the river canyon is formed by a sheer granite slope of Pyramid Peak which is the tallest mountain in the Crystal Range. It crests a little under 10,000 feet just inside the south boundary of the Desolation Wilderness.

Three miles farther is 42 Mile Camp and next door is Strawberry, now a winter sports area but formerly a popular stage and wagon stop.

The highway bends north from Strawberry to afford a spectacular view of Horsetail Falls cascading from Avalanche Lake into a granite ravine at the foot of Pyramid Peak. Off to the right of the road, across the river rises a cliff which is crowned by a promontory known as Lovers Leap. The old Bonanza Road ran deeper in the canyon here than the present highway. This stretch was known as Slippery Ford. It presented a difficult passage for the mule teams, especially during the spring run-off.

Highway 50 climbs above the 6,000 foot elevation before it spans Pyramid Creek at Twin Bridges. A dim trail leaves the west side of the creek for Horsetail Falls and Ropi Lake.

A short way up the road from Twin Bridges are several winter sports areas. The first is Edelweiss. Next is the Sierra Ski Ranch and then follows Little Norway, which was the site of Phillips Station in stagecoach days.

Just where Highway 50 begins a long hairpin turn to approach Echo Summit, a side road branches off to Firs Campground, the Echo Corrals pack station, and Echo Chalet. The latter resort has a store, cabins, and launching ramp at the east end of

*The Meyers Grade in January. The road is subject
to temporary closures during storms.*

the Echo Lakes. The Tahoe-Yosemite Trail from Lower Echo Lake affords the easiest hike into the Desolation Wilderness. A ferry service across both lakes saves backpackers three miles of walking.

Rimmed by glacier-polished granite, the Echo Lakes resemble the timberline rocky basin lakes found at much higher elevations in the Southern Sierra. Washo Indians used to fish the Echo Lakes. So did the "Lowery boys" who sold their catch to teamsters stopping at the 60 Mile House near Echo Summit. The Echo Lakes are tributary to Tahoe but, in 1876, a tunnel was drilled from the lower lake to the South Fork Canyon to provide additional water for mining.

Returning to the main road, we proceed to Echo Summit which was formerly known as Nevett's Summit and before then as Johnson's Pass. The elevation here is 7,377 feet. Very near the summit, a spur road leaves for the Echo Summit ski area. Just over the summit, the old Hawley Grade, now a rough trail, forks down to Upper Lake Valley.

Mostly mules were used on the Bonanza Road because oxen were too slow and horses were prone to injury on the punishing grades. The huge Washoe wagons carried up to fifteen tons of freight and were hauled by as many as eighteen pairs of mules. Eight miles in a day was good wagon time on the stretch between Placerville and Lake Valley. Often, the mules became mired in mud and there were flash floods. The mere appearance of a grizzly bear was enough to panic the teams. Another hazard was highwaymen. In 1864, a few days before Placerville celebrated Fourth of July, six men led by a Confederate officer, Captain R. Henry Ingram, staged a holdup to obtain gold for recruiting purposes.

Just around the 'Horn" at Echo Summit are several turn-outs which afford a distant view of Lake Tahoe and almost the full sweep of Lake Valley.

*The Upper Truckee River near the site of
Osgood's Tollhouse.*

Pines still blanket most of the valley, but here and there a grid of subdivision roads shows through the trees. Visible in the direction of the lake are two golf courses and the Lake Tahoe Airport.

The descent to Lake Valley is made on the new Meyers Grade. About halfway down, the old Meyers Grade angles off to the right. This road still bears the traffic when the main approach is blocked by a snow slide or washout. It was formerly known as Osgood's Grade, for Neamiah Osgood who maintained the route as a toll road.

At the foot of the grade, we leave the El Dorado National Forest just before US 50 spans the Upper Truckee River. Near this crossing was Osgood's Toll House. The log structure built in 1859 was washed away in 1911 when a dam on Lower Echo Lake burst, releasing 2,000 acre feet of water into the valley.

A short piece beyond the Truckee Crossing is the junction with State Highway 89. One-half mile farther is an agricultural checking station. This is on the outskirts of Tahoe Paradise, a nondescript collection of shops and real estate offices that was known as Meyers before the developers took it over. It was here that Tahoe's first settler, Martin Smith, built his inn and trading post in 1851. After the cabin was burned by outlaws in 1855, Smith and his partner, Jim Muir, built a new and larger structure. This was purchased by Ephraim "Yank" Clement in 1858 who sold it fifteen years later to George Henry Meyers, a native of Germany. In 1903, the inn was acquired by the Celio family. It was destroyed by fire in 1938. The site is marked by a plaque which memorializes the old hotel for its brief role as a remount station for the Pony Express.

A paved highway, known as the Pioneer Trail, leaves Tahoe Paradise for Stateline. This road is said to approximate the emigrant route blazed by "Cockeye" Johnson in 1848. It bypasses most of the congestion in South Lake Tahoe.

From Tahoe Paradise on US 50, it's four miles to the Tahoe

Driving up the Great Bonanza Road from Placerville,
the traveler obtains his first view of Lake Tahoe
at Echo Summit.

Valley shopping district. On this drive, we pass the airport, an ice skating rink, two wooded promontories known as Twin Peaks, and perhaps half a hundred motels.

At Tahoe Valley, there is a "Y" junction. US 50 veers right into the depths of South Lake Tahoe's neon jungle. State 89 bears left to approach the most beautiful area in the Tahoe Basin.

In the "Lucky" Baldwin era this was one of the busiest beaches at Tahoe.

IV THE TALLAC SHORE

Taking the Evening Sleeper at Oakland Pier you will arrive at Truckee the following morning, connecting with the new scenic railway to Lake Tahoe. On your arrival at Tahoe City, the new steel steamer 'Tahoe' will be waiting to take you to Tallac."— TALLAC—THE SUMMER RESORT OF THE WORLD by M. Lawrence & Co., 1902.

The mile-long stretch of Highway 89 between the "Y" junction at Tahoe Valley and Tallac Village is a broad boulevard lined with shiny new motels, shops, and service industries. Tallac Village sprawls just inside the corporate limits of South Lake Tahoe. Across this boundary is National Forest. Here the dwellings end, the road narrows, the woods close in, and the din of progress fades to a murmur.

Perhaps a quarter-mile inside the forest, a dim road leads off to the south. This spur runs to the Tahoe Mountain Campground, a special group camp for which reservations are required.

One mile farther, a road forks north to approach Pope Beach on the southernmost shore of Lake Tahoe. Here the white sand beach, the gin clear water, and the great expanse of the lake suggest a displaced bay of the Pacific Ocean. A tang of salt would complete the illusion but, instead, the breeze carries the pungent scent of pine and juniper.

On the warmest day in summer, you're apt to see more sunbathers than swimmers at Pope Beach because, even in the shallows, the water temperature at Tahoe stays on the cool side. In

Taylor Creek.

the forest behind the beach are dressing rooms and a large picnic area.

Proceeding west on Highway 89, it's a short drive to Camp Richardson, an old-style family resort, operated under special permit granted by the Forest Service. The facilities here include a store, lodge, cabins, campground, and large trailer park. The land hereabouts was homesteaded in 1872 by Matthew C. Gardner for whom Gardnerville, Nevada, is named. Gardner's interest was timber and, to log Lake Valley, he built a broad-gauged railway. The rolling stock included two locomotives acquired from the Virginia and Truckee Railway. These were hauled to the lake over Daggett Pass by teams of 24 horses and mules.

After Gardner went bankrupt in 1885, the land was bought by "Lucky" Baldwin, who eventually subdivided it for resorts and cottages. Camp Richardson was established in 1921 by A. L. Richardson, owner of the Pierce Arrow Stage that operated between the lake and Sacramento.

Not far from Camp Richardson is a nine-acre tract of lake frontage known as Valhalla. In 1970, the Forest Service acquired an option on this property with the help of the Lake Tahoe Land Reserve.

Next door to Camp Richardson is a pack station which has saddle stock for day rides.

A mile farther we come to a crossroads, Two roads on the right approach Kiva Beach and the Lake Tahoe Visitor Center. The beach is shaded by conifers and has forty picnic units.

Maps and information on the El Dorado National Forest may be obtained at the Visitor Center. This new structure is a hub of recreational activity on the Tallac Shore. Campfire programs, movies, sing fests, and slide lectures are featured at the amphitheatre. Group tours guided by Forest Service naturalists leave the center daily in summer. There are several self-guiding nature

41

The Tallac shore in winter. All but 250 feet of this
frontage is public land administered by the
El Dorado National Forest.

paths in the area. One of these leads to a stream profile chamber on Taylor Creek where you may enjoy a face-to-face confrontation with a trout or kokanee salmon.

Across Highway 89 from the Kiva Beach Drive, a road runs south to Fallen Leaf Lake. About one-half mile up this road is the Fallen Leaf Campground which has 210 tent and trailer sites. Fallen Leaf Lake may be approached from the campground on a self-guiding nature path known as the Moraine Trail.

The road continues to the lake where it skirts the east shore. Fallen Leaf is three miles long, almost a mile wide, 418 feet deep, and fringed by lush stands of lodgepole pine. The west shore is bound by a bare granite slope of Mount Tallac which crests 3,400 feet above the water. Geologists speak of Fallen Leaf as a "glacial trough end lake." It was hollowed out by a river of ice in Pleistocene times and impounded by a moraine of rocky debris left in the wake of the retreating glacier.

A legend credited to the Washo tells of an Indian brave who asked the Great Spirit for help in crossing the Sierra to Central Valley. The warrior was given a branch and told to drop a small piece of it on the ground when danger threatened. On top of the Carson Range, the Indian found himself pursued by a demon. In his haste to escape, the young brave broke off half the branch. This created Lake Tahoe, which provided an obstacle for the demon. But, the next time the demon appeared, the Indian took care to conserve his magic branch by dropping no more than a twig or single leaf. And so, in this manner, Fallen Leaf Lake and dozens of higher lakes in the Desolation Wilderness were born.

Some historians believe that Fallen Leaf was named for a Delaware chief who guided "Cockeye" Johnson on his explorations during the late 1840's and early 1850's. In "Lucky" Baldwin's day, Fallen Leaf was private trout water reserved for guests of the Tallac House. For a time, Baldwin operated a

The Tallac Shore in winter.

lumber mill on its shores. The lake today is open to public fishing and contains rainbow trout, Mackinaw trout, and kokanee salmon.

Two miles up the Fallen Leaf Road from State 89, an unpaved road branches east to connect with the steep, dusty spur to the tiny Angora Lakes. It's a four mile drive to the Angora Lookout where the road affords some dramatic views of Lake Valley and the Tahoe Basin. A mile or so beyond the lookout, the public road ends at a locked gate. There's a parking area close by. From here, it's less than a mile on foot to the resort at Upper Angora Lake which has a store, cabins, swimming beach, and rental skiffs. The elevation is 7,500 feet. Both lakes contain cutthroat trout.

Returning to the Fallen Leaf Road, we continue to Fallen Leaf Lodge at the south end of the lake. This resort, which includes a campground, boat rentals, and launching ramp, was established in 1905 by Professor William W. Price of Stanford University.

A trifle beyond the lodge, the road forks. A right turn takes us around to the west shore, which is dotted with summer cottages. The road ends at the start of the Cathedral Trail, said to be the steepest footpath in the Desolation Wilderness. To approach the summit of Mount Tallac, it gains 3,300 feet in elevation over a distance of five miles.

The other fork of the road follows Glen Alpine Creek about a mile up Glen Canyon to Lily Lake. This water contains three kinds of trout but is difficult to fish because of the lily pads. A little beyond the lake is a parking area. Here the road gives way to a dirt track that is private but open to pedestrians. You hike three-quarters of a mile to reach the meadow at Glen Alpine Springs. The mineral spring here was discovered by Nathan Gilmore in 1863 while he was searching for his cattle which had strayed from Fallen Leaf Lake.

The Gilmore family operated a popular spa at Glen Alpine for many years. The water from the springs was bottled and widely marketed as Glen Alpine Tonic Water. The Angora Lakes owe their name to a flock of goats which Gilmore brought up from the foothills for summer grazing.

An improved trail climbs from Glen Alpine to Lake Aloha and other trout waters in the Desolation Wilderness.

Returning to Highway 89, we proceed west one mile to the turn-off which leads to Baldwin Beach. On the way, we cross Taylor Creek and a nature trail which follows the stream 1½ miles to Fallen Leaf Lake.

Baldwin Beach has a lot of white sand but few trees. There are dressing rooms and some picnic units. An additional 900 feet of shoreline was added to the beach in 1971 through the efforts of a non-profit organization known as the Nature Conservancy.

Shortly after Ephraim "Yank" Clement, a fun-loving Forty-Niner from Vermont, sold his station in Lake Valley to George Meyers, he built a new hotel on the frontage at Baldwin and Kiva Beaches. A major attraction was the ballroom, which had its floor mounted on springs so as to give the dancers the sensation of "floating on air."

In 1880, "Yank's Place" became the stylish Tallac House after Clement sold out to Elias J. "Lucky" Baldwin. A shrewd operator in stocks and real estate, Baldwin had in 1874 unloaded his shares in the Ophir Mine to the Comstock banker William Sharon for the inflated price of $2.7 million. Baldwin's interest in Tahoe went back to 1853 when, as wagon captain of an emigrant train, he had made a camp in Lake Valley.

On the Fourth of July, 1889, the menu at Tallac featured stuffed chicken a l'Anglaise and Westphalia ham with Champagne sauce. Tallac was the last word at Tahoe, but Baldwin wasn't satisfied. In 1899, he built a new and grander Tallac

Highway 89 near the turn-off to Baldwin Beach. Copses of quaking aspen provide splashes of fall color in October.

House with such unheard-of refinements as steam heat, electric lights, and picture windows. Two years later, he added a large casino which included a ballroom, theatre, bowling alleys, and separate billiard parlors for ladies and gentlemen. Gambling was illegal, but Baldwin always seemed to know when the sheriff was coming.

Tallac was as self-sufficient as any feudal castle. It had its own vegetable gardens and 200 dairy cattle. On the grounds were facilities for such genteel sports as croquet, lawn tennis, and shuttlecock. For the more adventurous guests, there was sailing and horseback riding. There was a Washo tribal leader, "Indian Ben," who escorted hunting parties into the back country. The hotel's staff of fishing guides included Eric Von Stroheim who went on to fame and fortune in Hollywood.

In 1892, Baldwin acquired the beautiful steamer "Tallac." This was launched in 1890 as the "Nevada," but the vessel burned a year later. Baldwin had the hull lengthened to 85 feet and refitted the superstructure to accommodate forty passengers in splendid luxury.

The end of an era was signaled in 1906 when Mrs. Joseph Chansler drove her sporty new Simplex from Sacramento to Tallac in eight hours flat. The automobile was to bring increasing numbers of visitors to Tahoe who could not afford the fancy prices at Tallac.

And so, Tallac slowly withered on the vine, as did "Yank" Clement's less pretentious Cascade House which he had built next door to Tallac. Both Baldwin and Clement lived to a ripe old age. The Tallac House was razed by Baldwin's daughter in 1927. Now there's only a lovely beach and memories.

V EMERALD BAY

"The main body of the bay is of a deep blue our eyes have already become accustomed to, but the shoreline is a wonderful combination of jade and emerald that dances and scintillates as the breeze plays with the surface of the waters."—LAKE OF THE SKY by George Wharton James, 1915.

On this leg of the drive, Highway 89 climbs 600 feet above the lake to skirt the rim of Emerald Bay. The grade begins about three-quarters of a mile east of the Baldwin Beach turn-off. Shortly after you start up the switchbacks, a side road forks northeast to the Cascade Stables pack station.

A mile farther, near the apex of a long hairpin turn, a private road branches south to Cascade Lake which is one mile long and half a mile wide.

A San Francisco surgeon, Dr. Charles B. Brigham, purchased land at Cascade Lake in 1882 and gradually increased his holdings to 1,300 acres. For a time, the estate encompassed all of Cascade Lake and considerable frontage on Emerald Bay. Among Dr. Brigham's guests at his Cascade lodge were John Muir and Mark Twain. The novelist, John Steinbeck, served as caretaker for the estate in 1926. Cascade Lake provided a location for several motion pictures, including *Rose Marie, An American Tragedy,* and *A Place in the Sun.* The lake today is ringed with private homes.

It's a short way to the junction with the Eagle Point Road. This spur approaches two campgrounds in Emerald Bay State

Emerald Point. Looking north across Emerald Bay from Highway 89.

Park. There are 100 Class A sites perched high on the forested ridge which reaches out on the lake to Eagle Point.

The twin preserves, Emerald Bay State Park and D. L. Bliss State Park, cover 1,830 acres. Together they encompass the entire bayshore and several miles of frontage north of Emerald Point. The first gift of land was made in 1929 by the Bliss family who formerly controlled the mills at Glenbrook. In 1953, the Placerville lumberman, Harvey West, donated 176 acres on Emerald Bay.

The parks contain heavy stands of yellow, sugar, and Jeffrey pines mixed with white firs. There are some ancient gnarled Sierra junipers and scattered groves of incense cedar. Huckleberry oak grows in the brushy areas and Sierra maple in the lush streamside woodland of Eagle Creek. The timber is second growth but, here and there, you see a forest giant which escaped the selective cutting.

From the junction with the Eagle Point Road, the highway bears south on a ridgetop overlooking Cascade Lake. It's about a mile to Inspiration Point which commands a splendid view of Emerald Bay.

The bay was sculptured during the Ice Ages in much the same manner as Fallen Leaf Lake. The ridges which enclose the lower bay are glacial moraines. Everywhere the bay is deep except where it opens to the main lake between Emerald and Eagle Points. Here the lake steamers were prone to scrape bottom during years of low water.

The only approach to the bayshore was by water when the stage line tycoon, Ben Holladay, built a summer place on the bay in the early 1860's. Holladay's caretaker was British-born Captain Richard Barter, an eccentric recluse who whiled away the lonely winters carving scale models of barks and barkentines.

Barter was rowing back from a visit to the saloons at Tahoe

*Fanette Island in Emerald Bay is the only true island
on the lake.*

City one night in the winter of 1870 when a sudden squall caused his boat to capsize. Struggling in the icy water, Barter managed to right the skiff but was too exhausted to bail it out. To keep himself from freezing, he lay in the flooded boat with only his face above water. From time to time, he fortified himself by taking a nip of whiskey and screaming into the gale, "Richard Barter never surrenders."

The next morning, Barter managed to bail the boat and row to Emerald Bay where he amputated his frozen toes with a hunting knife. A few years later, Barter drowned when his boat overturned off Rubicon Point.

Across Highway 89 from Inspiration Point is Bayview. Here there's a resort with cabins, a Forest Service guard station, and the Bayview Campground which has 18 sites for tent campers. A steep horse trail out of Bayview approaches the popular Velma Lakes Basin.

Beyond Bayview, the highway hugs a nearly vertical slope of the Maggie Peaks. This granite incline rises from the head of Emerald Bay to crest 2,400 feet above the lake. When the roadbed was being blasted in 1913, the lake steamers brought tourists to watch the tons of rock hurtling down the cliffs.

Snow closes this stretch of Highway 89 for weeks at a time in winter. It had to be completely rebuilt following a massive landslide in 1956. About this time, the state proposed to bridge Emerald Bay and ring the lake with expressways. The scheme was hooted down by Tahoe residents.

A mile up the road from Bayview is the Eagle Falls Campground, reserved for use by hikers and tent campers. The Velma Lakes and other waters in Desolation Wilderness may be approached from here on an excellent footpath. It's a steep one-mile hike to the nearest lake but just an easy stroll to a lovely waterfall on Eagle Creek.

A little farther up the highway is Emerald Lookout. The ruins

Emerald Bay—the view from Inspiration Point.

of a stone tea house on Fannette Island are visible from the parking lot. A rocky, dome-like islet, Fannette is the only true island on Tahoe.

A trail from Emerald Lookout drops down to the inlet of Eagle Creek on Emerald Bay. The frontage here was purchased in 1928 to provide a summer estate for the wealthy heiress, Josephine Lora Knight.

Emerald Bay recalled for Mrs. Knight a Norwegian fjord she had seen on her travels through Scandinavia. So, with the help of scholars, she designed a summer home that was an exact replica of an ancient Norse fortress, circa 800 A.D. No nails were used in the construction. The planking was joined by wooden pegs. Faithful to tradition, the sod roof was sowed with grass so the livestock would have a place to forage when the fortress was snowed in or under siege.

Now state property, "Vikingsholm" has 38 rooms furnished with antique furniture and fine tapestries acquired by Mrs. Knight on her trips abroad. The lower floor is open to visitors in summer. Families picnic on the front lawn which abuts a wading beach. A steep trail leaves the grounds to follow Eagle Creek to the Middle Falls.

Another footpath, the 4½-mile Rubicon Trail, runs along the shore to Calawee Cove at the north end of D. L. Bliss State Park. About halfway between "Vikingsholm" and Emerald Point, the trail passes an isolated campground with twenty improved sites.

The main entrance to Bliss State Park lies approximately two miles up the highway from Emerald Lookout. The park drive approaches three campgrounds. Two trails which leave Camp No. 1 connect with the Rubicon Trail. Near Camp No. 2, a self-guiding nature path tours a rocky area where dwarf sugar pines grow. Off this trail, you see the 130-ton "Balancing Rock" perched precariously on an eroded pedestal of granite. Camp

No. 3 fronts Lester and Calawee Beaches. It's a short walk from here to Rubicon Point, described by Tahoe historian, Edward B. Scott, as "a replica of the face of Yosemite's Half Dome with water against it."

On a sunny day, the water around Rubicon Point reflects a dark intense blue because the drop-off is extreme. Hardly a quarter-mile from shore the lake is 1,200 feet deep. The steamer captains used to give their passengers a thrill by navigating within a few yards of Rubicon Point. Seen from a boat, the rocks around the point assume fanciful shapes. Most have local names, such as Frog Rock, Hen and Chickens, Sleeping Lady, Old King Cole, and the Gladiator.

VI DESOLATION WILDERNESS

"The trouble with Desolation—the cause of the congestion—is that it is too small, too pretty, and too easy to get into. This friendly eight-by-twelve section of the Sierra Crest is only three-and-a-half hours from San Francisco, two hours from Sacramento, and twenty minutes from South Lake Tahoe."—DESOLATION WILDERNESS by John S. Wood, 1971

The Desolation Wilderness contains some splendid scenery and the largest concentration of Sierra trout waters north of Sonora Pass. Besides some fair-sized creeks, there are roughly one hundred lakes situated at elevations from 7,000 to 9,000 feet. Many of the lakes are found clustered in rocky basins. A few nestle in lofty glacial cirques. Others lie deep in forested canyons, strung out like a necklace of beads.

At least eighty of the lakes contain rainbow, brown, cutthroat, or Eastern brook trout. As many as three different trout species may co-exist in a single lake. Alta Morris Lake contains golden trout, Stony Ridge Lake has Mackinaw, and, in recent years, some shallow tarns have been planted with Arctic grayling.

There is an elaborate network of trails. Most of these were blazed by early cattlemen and fur trappers when the region was known as the Rubicon Wilderness. In 1931, the Forest Service classified 41,383 acres here as "primitive" and called this roadless enclave the Desolation Valley Wild Area. The present name was given in 1969 when the area closed to motor vehicles was increased to 63,469 acres and made a unit of the National Wilderness system.

The heaviest traffic of day hikers, backpackers, and horse

Plump, pan-sized Eastern brook trout are abundant in many of the Desolation Lakes.

parties occurs from Fourth of July weekend through Labor Day. Spring wildflowers still afford some gorgeous color in July but fade in August when the quality of lake fishing is unreliable.

At most lakes, angling peaks twice in a season. The first peak occurs in May, June, or July, whenever the ice melts. After the "summer doldrums," the action begins to pick up again around mid-September as the surface waters cool.

The trails at the higher elevations in early season are likely to be snowbound. Streams swollen by snow-melt may be difficult, if not dangerous, to ford before July or August. There is apt to be some lovely weather in autumn but on the warmest day you may expect the mercury to drop below freezing as soon as the sun sets.

There's summer fishing in about a dozen streams, including the Rubicon River. The latter was among the most celebrated trout waters in California before it was impounded to supply hydroelectric stations of the Sacramento Utility District. An aid to fishing are the little check dams constructed at lake outlets to maintain stream levels through the dry months. Most of these were built by the Mount Ralston Fish Planting Club, founded in 1925 by summer residents at Echo Lake.

In Forty-Niner days, most of the Desolation lakes were barren of fish. The first stocking was a volunteer effort by ranchers and sportsmen. The trout collected in milk cans were packed in by mule. The state took over this chore in 1931. Presently, a few lakes contain self-supporting populations of brook or brown trout. The rest must be replenished every few years by aerial drops from state tanker planes. The little hatchery-reared fingerlings which survive this rough treatment and grow to size are no less wild than the native trout.

The wilderness area fills a ragged rectangle six to eight miles wide and fifteen miles long where the highest peaks crest a trifle under 10,000 feet. The main divide of the Sierra crests just in-

*Snow may linger on the higher slopes of the Desolation
peaks through most of summer.*

side the east boundary of the wilderness. The west boundary encloses the summit of the Crystal Range.

Separating the Crystal Range from the main Sierra Divide is a deep glacier-excavated trench. The northern two-thirds of this trough is occupied by Rockbound Valley. The southern part is filled by the Desolation Valley which the pioneers spoke of as the "Devil's Basin."

Ground cover is sparse and there are only scattered patches of forest in the granite wasteland of the Desolation Valley. But here is concentrated the densest grouping of lakes. Lake Aloha, the largest body of water, was a chain of little tarns before it was impounded by a power dam.

A short but rugged hike north of Lake Aloha, just over Mosquito Pass, is Clyde Lake. From this golden trout water, the Rubicon River flows nine miles through Rockbound Valley north to Rubicon Reservoir. There's more timber in Rockbound Valley but the lakes are fairly scattered and too remote for an overnight hike. The easiest approach to these waters is from Loon Lake, situated just outside the northwest corner of the Wilderness. It's a thirty-mile drive on a road which leaves US 50 at Riverton. Another way to get to Loon Lake is on the Wentworth Springs Road out of Georgetown.

The USFS campground at Wrights Lake provides a convenient base for the small but productive trout lakes which dot the west slope of the Crystal Range. You motor eight miles to Wright Lake on a rough unpaved spur which leaves Highway 50 five miles east of Kyburz.

The lakes tributary to Fallen Leaf Lake may be approached from the Glen Alpine trailhead.

A lush forest of red fir and lodgepole pine fills the northeast corner of Desolation Wilderness. Here a trail out of Meeks Bay runs to a chain of lovely lakes in the Phipps Peak area. From the

61

Azure Lake is one of more than 80 glacial lakes in the Desolation Wilderness which contain trout.

uppermost lake, you may hike over Phipps Pass to the Velma Lakes Basin and return to Highway 89 on the Eagle Falls Trail.

Until a few summers ago, you could walk into the Desolation country and not go far before you arrived at a lake where you could camp and fish in perfect solitude. Now, to find solitude, you must aim for one of the more remote waters and schedule your trip to avoid a weekend or major holiday.

The growing pressure on the Desolation area coincides with a phenomenal rise in the popularity of backpacking. This has had an impact everywhere in the Sierra back country but it is felt most keenly in the more accessible areas which invite short over-night hikes.

It's a challenge for the Forest Service how to protect these areas from overuse. The Desolation Wilderness had 36,000 visitor days recorded in 1966. The number rose to 48,000 in 1967 and 73,500 in 1969. On one day in 1970, more than 500 hikers signed the register at the Echo Lakes trailhead.

To cope with the crush, the Forest Service assigns several "wilderness rangers" to patrol the more heavily used areas and pick up after sloppy campers. But more serious than the litter problem is the threat of pollution at some lakes. There are camping spots where the ground has become so compacted by the press of people that the trees are dying. Trails subject to heavy traffic by horse parties have become badly eroded.

Some observers blame this damage on poor management by the Forest Service. For example, in 1968 the sum of $72,000 was spent to reconstruct nine miles of the trail which runs from Echo Lake through the Desolation Valley. Seasoned hikers refer to the new trail as a "freeway." The effect of the improvement has been to encourage "bunching up" at some of the most popular lakes.

Beginning in 1971, visitors to the Desolation Wilderness and all other areas of back country in California's National Forests

*Lake Genevieve is approached from Highway 89 on the
Meeks Creek Trail. Brown trout and Eastern brook
trout may be caught here. The lake teems with
red side minnows.*

must possess a wilderness permit. This replaces the old fire permit that was formerly issued. No fee is charged but a wilderness permit must be applied for in advance of each trip. The permits are issued by ranger stations of the National Forest in which the trailhead is located. There is speculation the Forest Service may eventually employ the new permit system to limit attendance in the more heavily used areas. A fee may be charged and advance reservations required.

It would relieve pressure on the Desolation area if more back country around Tahoe was added to the National Wilderness system. But so great is the charm of the Desolation lakes that some controls, such as a ban on hunting and horse travel, may be necessary to preserve this gem of the Sierra for future generations.

There are several guide books which provide detailed information on the Desolation lakes and trails. Of these, the most complete exposition is found in the "Desolation Wilderness" by Robert S. Wood. This book lists all the lakes and includes an excellent chapter on fishing.

The Meeks Creek Trail approaches a chain of trout-filled lakes in the Phipps Peak area.

VII SUGAR PINE POINT

"Six miles from Tahoe (City) over a beautiful road, we reach Sugar Pine Point, a spur of mountains covered with a splendid forest of sugar pine, the most valuable timber for all uses found on the Pacific Coast."—NEW OVERLAND TOURIST AND PACIFIC COAST GUIDE by George A. Crofutt, 1884.

North from D. L. Bliss State Park, the highway loses several hundred feet in elevation on a hasty descent to the lakeside at Rubicon Bay. Here the frontage is private and crowded with summer homes.

From park headquarters, it's roughly five miles to Meeks Bay. This wooded inlet of Meeks Creek was a favorite camping place of the Washo because of its sheltered location on the south side of Sugar Pine Point.

It's recorded that "Meeks & Co." cut wild hay near the bay in 1860. The ranchers, George Thomas and James A. Murphy, homesteaded a cow camp on the bayshore in 1878. A few years later, the area was logged by the Carson and Tahoe Lumber and Fluming Company of Glenbrook. When the land was put up for sale in 1919, Oswald Kehlet established the 1,200-acre Meeks Bay Resort which is still in business.

The resort includes a lodge, theatre, store, cabins, campground, trailer park, marina, launching ramp, and perhaps the finest swimming beach at Tahoe. One by one, such pleasant rustic resorts have faded from the Tahoe scene, forced to liquidate by high maintenance costs and the tax rise which results from the spread of subdivisions. The Meeks Bay establishment was owned and operated by the same family up through 1969. Then,

Private pier at Tahoe Pines. There are 439 piers and over 50 marinas on the lake.

in 1970, the Macco Corporation announced it planned to build 1,744 condominium units on the land. But there was no construction before the Penn Central, of which the Macco Corporation is subsidiary, found itself in financial difficulty and the land was offered for sale. In the spring of 1971, the League to Save Lake Tahoe purchased 649 acres of the resort, including 3,000 feet of frontage on Meeks Bay.

The League to Save Lake Tahoe is a non-profit organization composed largely of Tahoe business and professional people. It will hold the land in trust until the Forest Service can obtain funds to buy it. Meanwhile, the Meeks Bay Resort continues to operate.

An unpaved road leaves Highway 89 opposite the Meeks Bay Theatre. This spur runs 1½ miles southwest to the northern terminus of the Tahoe-Yosemite Trail. From the roadhead, it's a three-mile hike to forest-fringed Lake Genevieve. This is the first in a chain of good fishing lakes which dot the Phipps Peak section of the Desolation Wilderness.

At Meeks Bay, there is a pack station which affords "spot" and guided trips into the wilderness.

From the Meeks Bay Theatre, the drive is short to the south boundary of Sugar Pine Point State Park. This is a new preserve which includes the former summer estate of Isaias W. Hellman. The park encompasses 3,174 acres of forested land, much of which is flat or nearly so. There's more than a mile of shoreline, edged with some attractive beaches and a 200-foot pier. The camping area has 175 improved sites. The park stays open all year. On winter weekends, the park rangers conduct nature walks over the snow.

The park's stately sugar pines are mixed with firs, cedars, and Jeffrey pines. The native wildlife includes a variety of small mammals, such as chipmunks, squirrels, and long-tail weasels. Food left unprotected overnight is certain to be raided by rac-

Toplining for rainbow trout off Meeks Bay.

coons if it does not attract a bear. Among the many kinds of birds seen at the point is the colorful Western tanager.

Brook, brown, and rainbow trout are found in General Creek which runs three miles through the heart of the park. The stream was named for "General" William Phipps, a hard-bitten veteran of the Indian Wars when he moved up from Georgetown in 1860 to pioneer a homestead on Sugar Pine Point.

Phipps supported himself at Tahoe mainly by hunting and fishing. In time, he worked up a business selling trout eggs which were much in demand by fish hatcheries and by sportsmen for use as bait. This enterprise was hurt when the California Fish Commission visited Tahoe in 1883 to investigate complaints that trout were becoming scarce in the lake.

At Sugar Pine Point, the delegation discovered 900 brood fish which Phipps had penned in a pool on General Creek. Sputtering with rage, Phipps fired his twin Colt revolvers in the air but the Commission was not impressed. They gave him 48 hours to release the fish or go to jail.

One of two cabins built by Phipps still stands near the mouth of General Creek. Built of split logs, it is wonderfully preserved.

Phipps lived in splendid isolation until a wagon road out of Tahoe City was completed to the point in 1882. A few years later, Phipps sold his land to Captain W. "Billy" Lapham, who built on it a hotel known as "Bellevue." For a brief period, this was a property of the Wells-Fargo Express Company. The hotel gained prestige when the wealthy financier, M. H. de Young, established a summer place next door to the resort.

Near General Creek, not far from the Phipps Cabin, stands a gabled mansion built in 1903 for the San Francisco banker, Isaias Hellman. During summer, the house is open to visitors on Wednesday, Saturday, and Sunday afternoons. On the grounds is an ancient juniper tree, nearly five feet thick, which John Muir described as "the largest and finest in the Sierra."

*Most of the main roads in the Tahoe area
are kept open even after heavy snows.*

The Desolation back country may be approached from Sugar Pine Point on the Lower General Creek Trail. It's five miles from the campground to a junction with the Upper General Creek Trail, which runs south to link up with the Tahoe-Yosemite Trail.

The north boundary of the park abuts Tahoma on McKinney Bay. This summer colony has nine resorts. The area takes its name from the Hotel Tahoma built here in 1916 by Joe Bishop, a prosperous San Francisco chimney sweep. The subdivision west of the highway dates back to 1925 when land here was sold to Lon Chaney and other Hollywood personalities.

Next door to Tahoma across the El Dorado-Placer County line was Chamber's Lodge, described by David Chambers as an "old-fashioned mountain inn, but not a dressy place." It was the oldest operating hotel at Tahoe before it was torn down in 1970 to make way for a high-rise condominium development. About 250 units were planned to sell for upwards to $125,000 each. But the project was defeated by summer home owners who complained to the County Planning Commission that it would "urbanize" the shoreline and block their view of the lake.

On the Sierra crest due west of the lodge site, the cattlemen, John Wren and John W. McKinney, established a hay ranch in 1861. A year later, McKinney, an ex-miner from Missouri, moved down to the lakeshore where he started a rustic resort known as the "Hunter's Retreat."

McKinney's place prospered partly because of its location at the terminus of an old Indian trail that ran to Georgetown. This trail was trod in the 1860's by mule trains packing freight for the Comstock. From McKinney's dock, the supplies were ferried to Glenbrook on the schooner, "Iron Duke."

The McKinney-Rubicon Springs Road which leaves State 89 a little north of Tahoma approximates the route of the old trail as far as Miller Lake. The pavement ends on this spur about a

*Some historians believe the Rubicon River was named
in analogy to Caesar's crossing of the Rubicon. The
stream presented a difficult crossing on the old
emigrant trail from Tahoe to Georgetown.*

mile from the highway. Three miles farther, between Lily and Miller Lakes, it spans the Sierra Crest at Burton Pass. Just north of Miller Lake, there is a junction with the Miller Lake Jeep Trail which runs to Wentworth Springs. The trail is named for James Harrison Miller, a pioneer who ran sheep in Miller Meadows.

In July, a large turn-out of four wheel drive enthusiasts navigates the boulder-strewn Miller Trail on the annual Jeepers Jamboree. An overnight bivouac is made at Rubicon Springs where Tahoe pioneers claimed the carbonated mineral water tasted "better than whiskey." Here, deep in the rugged canyon of the Rubicon River, the brothers John and George Hunsucker founded a cattle ranch in 1867.

In 1880, the Hunsuckers began a prosperous business merchandising Rubicon Spring water. There was no way to transport the water except by mule train until 1886 when young Mrs. Sierra Nevada Phillips Clark bought the land, supervised construction of a sixteen-room hotel, equipped it with horsehair furniture, and persuaded El Dorado County to build the Rubicon Road.

Guests who survived the jolting ride in the "Rubicon Flyer" often found they were required to sleep outside in a meadow because the hotel was full. The spa was enormously popular with wealthy Comstockers, partly because they esteemed Mrs. Clark as "the best cook in the Sierra." After the dishes were cleared, she would put in several hours at the piano for dances and song fests.

Mrs. Clark, known to her friends as "Vade," was the daughter of the innkeeper who founded Phillips Station on the Great Bonanza Road.

Only ruins remain of the old resort and the river here is much changed since the impoundment of Rubicon Reservoir, several miles upstream at Onion Flat. It's a 6½-mile drive to the springs

*North of the Desolation Wilderness, the Rubicon River
enters a rugged canyon from which it does not emerge
before it joins the American River.*

by way of the Miller Lake Jeep Trail. Hikers may shorten the distance 1½ miles by taking a cut-off on the trail. The Rubicon Road is not fit for travel in a conventional car beyond the junction southwest of Miller Lake with the Richardson Lake Road. Hikers may walk the latter road one-half mile to approach the start of the Upper General Creek Trail.

Rubicon Springs and several resorts which sprang up on McKinney Bay gave John McKinney's "Hunter's Retreat" some lively competition. To discourage travel to the springs, a large rattlesnake alleged to have been killed in the Rubicon Canyon was placed on exhibit in McKinney's saloon. But right next door to McKinney's was the popular Moana Villa Hotel, situated on land homesteaded by Augustus Colwell in 1867. Here, during the 1920's, the colorful evangelist, Aimee Semple McPherson, held revivals in the hotel dance hall.

McKinney, who could neither read nor write, was a gregarious, warm-hearted person, always short of funds because he was reluctant to press for payment of monies owed to him. For lack of $600 cash to pay a liquor bill, he lost his resort in 1892 to William Westhoff, a hard-nosed whiskey drummer from San Francisco. A broken man, McKinney retired to dwell in a bathhouse near Tahoe City.

In 1897, the Glenbrook House, a 2½-story inn where many Comstockers put up for the night, was barged across the lake to McKinney's old place. The inn became known as Chamber's Lodge when David Chambers bought the resort in 1920.

A mile up Highway 89 from the Chamber's Lodge property is Homewood, a resort and summer home development that was settled in the 1880's. Here is a pack station and two winter sports areas, the Tahoe Ski Bowl and Homewood Ski Area. The latter has a chair lift which operates in summer to afford a superlative view of the lake.

Next door to Homewood on opposing sides of Blackwood

El Dorado National Forest sign on Rubicon Canyon Trail.

Creek are Tahoe Pines and Idlewild. This area was homesteaded in 1863 by Homer Craig Blackwood, a Forty-Niner from North Carolina. Blackwood and his partner William A. Barker ran cattle on the headwaters of Blackwood Creek.

Idlewild in the Gay Nineties was the residence of multi-millionaires. The most imposing estate was that of Judge Edwin B. Crocker, who was legal counsel for the Southern Pacific Railroad. A leader in the smart set at Idlewild was Crocker's daughter, the princess Alexander Galitzine, who recounted her adventures in "I'd Do It Again" and the sensational, "Paula Loves Pearls."

Frederick C. Kohl bought the Crocker Estate in 1905. In 1926, it was acquired by the San Francisco tycoon, Herbert Fleishhacker, Sr. There was subdivision in the 1930's when Henry J. Kaiser purchased a large tract of frontage on the south side of Blackwood Creek. Here a crew of 300 workmen drained a marsh, filled it with loam and gravel, and built Kaiser's palatial Fleur du Lac, all in twenty-nine days.

An era ended when the Kaiser family disposed of Fleur du Lac. At last report, a San Jose plumbing contractor was planning to build condominiums on the property.

At Idlewild on the north side of Blackwood Creek, a pinnacle, known as Eagle Rock, towers 250 feet above the highway. This promontory served the Washo as a lookout for spotting game.

A little farther is the Kaspian Picnic Area of the Tahoe National Forest. The shaded picnic sites overlook a quarter-mile of public beach.

From Kaspian, a Forest Service road branches west up Blackwood Canyon to span the Sierra crest at Barker Pass. This highly scenic road affords a dusty approach to recreation areas at French Meadows Reservoir.

Meeks Bay theatre in January.

VIII TAHOE CITY

"There are two tiny steamboats on Lake Tahoe. Every morning one lies at the little wharf opposite the hotel and rings its miniature bell and whistles its gentle whistle; but it will wait while the head waiter puts up more lunch or the bridegroom runs back for the forgotten shawl."—BITS OF TRAVEL AT HOME by H. H., 1887

At mid-century, a stranger motoring around Tahoe could readily perceive a difference in style and atmosphere at opposite ends of the lake.

With the demise of Tallac, the South Shore had opted in favor of simple rustic resorts catering to families of middle income. Then, as traffic swelled on Highway 50, the resorts were displaced by conventional motels more suited for the transient custom of the Stateline casinos.

The North Shore was reluctant to forsake the carriage trade. Well into the Sixties, it retained a measure of old-fashioned elegance as represented by the aging Tahoe Tavern and Brockway Hot Springs Hotel. There were fewer motels and the casinos at Crystal Bay had a more exclusive air about them.

Now the difference between the two shores is less apparent. The North Shore still has expensive places but the elegance is gone. Brockway and the Tahoe Tavern properties are recreational subdivisions. Tahoe City, Kings Beach, and Crystal Bay can nearly match the blatant commercialism of South Lake Tahoe.

Pollution, high density, and traffic problems threaten to drive away the affluent. Yet there is little here for vacationers who must economize. All but a tiny fraction of the North Shore is private. The impressive sounding Tahoe State Recreation Area is a wee triangle of piney woods walled in by summer homes and a Safeway super market.

There's hardly an acre of frontage on the North Shore which hasn't felt the tread of a bulldozer. In 1970, one of the last natural areas was approved for subdivision by the Placer County Board of Supervisors. This is Ward Creek Canyon which opens to the lake about a mile and a quarter north of Idlewild.

In 1863, Augustus Saxon, a cattleman from Placerville, built a sawmill on Ward Creek that was powered by a water wheel 54 feet high. A few years later, Saxon contracted with Colis P. Huntington of the Central Pacific to deliver railway ties to Truckee. This deal nearly ruined Saxon. He had counted on floating the timbers down the Truckee River but the green wood sank and piled up behind the rocks. So Saxon was forced to deliver the ties by horse and wagon, a costly undertaking which ate up most of his profit.

The Saxon Mill closed shortly after a forest fire ravaged Tahoe's northwest shore in 1877. There was more lumbering around the turn of the century when a spur of the Lake Tahoe Railway was extended to Ward Creek. Afterwards, there was subdivision which gave rise to the neighboring summer colonies of Sunnyside and Tahoe Park. Here logged-over waterfront lots, measuring 50 by 100 feet, sold for as little as $50.

Off Highway 89, a trifle north of Ward Creek, is the William Kent USFS Campground. There are 95 campsites, including 70 units with space for trailers.

Two miles farther, we pass the former site of the Tahoe Tavern built in 1901 for the Bliss family on a lovely flat shaded by virgin timber. Throughout its existence, the Tavern was the most prestigious resort on the lake, boasting all the attributes of a first class metropolitan hotel.

Up through 1924, the Tavern provided a terminal for the

sleek lake steamers and picturesque little trains of the Lake Tahoe Railway and Transportation Company. The latter firm was organized by the Bliss family in the 1890's after they evacuated Glenbrook and bought out the Donner Lumber and Boom Company at Tahoe City.

A joy to behold were the miniature wood-burning locomotives of the Lake Tahoe Railway with their jaunty balloon stacks and boilers of polished brass. Among the notables who delighted in the sixteen-mile ride up the Truckee Canyon were Henry Ford and Thomas B. Edison.

At Tahoe Tavern, the trains would move out on a pier which projected one-eighth mile from shore. Here the conductor and brakeman would don pursers' caps before transferring their passengers aboard the steamers "Tahoe" and "Nevada." The latter vessel was known as the "Tallac" when it was owned by "Lucky" Baldwin.

The "Tahoe" was built to order for Duane Bliss in San Francisco. The hull, boiler, and other components were shipped by rail to Carson City and transported thence by mule team over Spooner Summit to Glenbrook. Launched in 1896, the vessel was widely acclaimed as an object of grace and beauty. The steel hull, which was divided into eight water-tight compartments, measured 168 feet, 9 inches long, with a beam of less than eighteen feet and a draft of only six feet.

The engines were capable of 1200 horsepower. The interior of the 100-foot deckhouse was fitted with expensive hardwoods and Brussels carpets. There was easily space for 200 passengers. The dining room below deck could seat 30 persons.

The "Tahoe" and "Nevada" made regular runs around the lake, stopping at McKinney's, Tallac, Bijou, and other landings for the transfer of passengers and freight.

Across Highway 89 from the Tavern grounds is Granlibakken, the first winter sports area at the lake. It was developed a

Stage for Truckee leaving Tahoe City's Grand Central Hotel on a summer day in 1880. From the collection at the California State Library.

few years after the Southern Pacific leased the Lake Tahoe Railway from the Bliss interests for annual payment of one silver dollar. In 1926, the Southern Pacific tore up the narrow gauge track and replaced it with standard gauge to provide through overnight service from Oakland to Tahoe City. The "Snowball Specials" which operated on weekends and holidays brought crowds of skiers to the lake.

Just north of the Tavern site at Outlet Point was the summer cottage of Louisa Keyser, a Washo who crafted exquisite ceremonial baskets, each with an original design. Many were sold to tourists for a trifling fraction of their true value, estimated upwards to $10,000 each. Examples of Louisa Keyser's work are found in several institutions, including the Nevada State Museum at Carson City.

We approach Tahoe City on the Fanny Bridge which spans the Truckee outlet a few yards below the watergate. Visitors gather on the bridge when traffic permits to observe the large trout which frequent the stream here. No angling is permitted for 1,000 feet below the dam.

Tahoe City. The name has a ring to it which belies a modest waterfront village wholly dependent on the passing motorist and a part-time population of "second home" owners. The town is backed up against a slope of Mount Watson, an ancient volcano subsidiary to Mount Pluto. The business district is centered around the "Y" junction where Highway 89 connects with Nevada Route 28.

The north side of Tahoe City abuts a nine-hole golf course. The lakeside is fronted by several marinas and a picnic ground, known as the Tahoe Commons which was confirmed by Act of Congress in 1867. The town is hardly picturesque, thanks to a profusion of neon signs and modern store fronts but a few of the old landmarks remain. There is Hunt's Gift Shop, built in 1909, which stands opposite a tree located in the middle of Nevada 28.

*Piers in Tahoe City area. The longest pier projects from
the site of the old Tahoe Tavern, now a
recreational sub-division.*

The Tahoe Inn was constructed on the site of William Pomin's historic Tahoe House immediately after the latter structure burned to the ground in 1934. The former SP Depot presently serves as an Episcopalian Church.

Settlement came to Tahoe City shortly after John A. Huntington completed the Truckee-Tahoe Toll Road up the river canyon in 1860. This was a rough track scarcely wide enough to support a stage coach. Beginning in 1862, hay cut in Squaw Valley was shipped from the roadhead to the South Shore on the schooner "Iron Duke." About this time, Homer D. Burton's "Edith Batty" began delivering mail around the lake. The little seven-ton sloop required a week to complete the circuit.

Another early enterprise was commercial fishing. But logging was the mainstay of the settlement when M. L. King completed his Tahoe City Hotel in 1864. During this year, the steamer "Governor Blaisdell" paid its first call to the north shore. The chunky little side wheeler occasionally carried passengers and freight but was mainly used for hauling logs. Regular passenger service was inaugurated shortly after Captain "Billy" Lapham's 92-foot side wheeler, the "Governor Stanford," was launched in 1872.

Boat tickets were purchased at Tahoe City's Custom House, a 24-hour waterfront saloon with two billiard parlors, one of which was reserved for ladies.

In 1871, the Tahoe City Hotel was enlarged, refurbished, and renamed the Grand Central Hotel. Graced by black walnut furniture and an $800 kitchen range, for some years it was the most celebrated inn between Sacramento and Virginia City.

The same year the Grand Central opened its doors, a brilliant Russian-born engineer, Alexis W. Von Schmidt, announced his plan to deliver water from Tahoe to the San Francisco Bay Area. Von Schmidt had built a low dam at the Truckee outlet near the site of the present watergate. From here, he proposed to run an aqueduct which would pass beneath the Sierra crest by way of a railroad tunnel. The latter would reduce the elevation of the Central Pacific by 1,000 feet and eliminate seven miles of track.

But the railroad had already run its line over Donner Summit. There was little support for the plan in San Francisco and violent opposition from ranchers in Nevada.

Von Schmidt finally gave up, but this was only the opening gun in a complex struggle for Tahoe's water which continues into the present and involves Indians, lake dwellers, resort interests, public utilities, a score of government agencies, and farmers on both sides of the California-Nevada line.

Von Schmidt sold his dam to a firm subsidiary to the Central Pacific and headed by Mark Hopkins and Leland Stanford. This was the Donner Lumber and Boom Company which had acquired a twenty-year franchise from the California legislature to float logs down the Truckee.

The present watergate was built in 1909. On the south bank is a log cabin, the former residence of the gate keeper. For some time, the Chamber of Commerce and North Lake Tahoe Historical Society have sought to obtain the site for a park and museum. At last report, the Sierra Power Company was willing to dedicate it to the public on condition a nearby business was eliminated so there would be no commercial exploitation of the park.

However, on the north side of the outlet, the power company proposes to build a 48-unit condominium to replace a motel that burned down during a fire drill in the spring of 1971. This move has sparked lively opposition from a local group known as "Save the People's Beach" which seeks to have the frontage added to the Tahoe Commons.

IX LAKE FOREST
TO BROCKWAY

"A ride in a row-boat, one pleasant morning, was particularly enjoyable. We went over to Cornelian Bay, and along the first part of the way the lake was as calm as a summer evening. The water which dripped from the oars, falling into the lake, made little circlets which the sun at once converted into rainbows."—
TWO YEARS IN CALIFORNIA by Mary Cone, 1876

East of Tahoe City, what used to be a loose chain of charming summer colonies has grown and fused into a lakeside megalopolis which bristles with new construction. Tall pines and firs still soften the worst excesses of high density, except at Kings Beach. Here the forest falls apart in a dazzling explosion of commercial pop art.

On the outskirts of Tahoe City, about two-thirds of a mile from the "Y" junction, is the pint-sized Tahoe State Recreation Area. The campground here has 39 Class "A" units and adjoins a tiny beach from which projects a fishing pier and one-lane boat ramp.

A mile farther on Highway 28 is the county-maintained Lake Forest Campground, a project of the California Wildlife Conservation Board. There are twenty campsites not suitable for trailers and a three-lane boat ramp. Next door is the Tahoe Station of the U. S. Coast Guard.

An early settler at Lake Forest was Homer D. Burton, who owned the "Edith Batty" and "Pride of the Lake." These were among the first sailing vessels to navigate Tahoe. In the 1880's, Burton established his Island Farm and Hotel which was a special favorite of the clergy. Burton, a cheerful extrovert, was im-

Tahoe's north shore fairly bristles with private piers. Here is Carnelian Bay with Dollar Point in the background.

mensely proud of his home-grown turnips and of his prowess as an angler.

In an age before movies, radio, and television, it behooved the successful resort manager to be adept at telling stories. Burton was a marvelous raconteur and nobody seemed to mind that most of his yarns were obvious fabrications. But, when Burton related how he caught a monster 29¾-pound trout in Tahoe and gave it to Ulysses S. Grant, anyone who raised an eyebrow was shown a letter from the President to prove the tale was true.

From Lake Forest, the highway climbs a few hundred feet above the lake to cross Dollar Point. This promontory was named for the shipping tycoon, "Captain" Robert S. Dollar, who bought land here in 1927. Earlier, it was known as "Lousy Point," some say because it was inhabited by a settler who changed his clothes only once a year.

When James Lick offered to donate a million dollars for construction of an observatory, the engineer-surveyor, Alexis Von Schmidt, was quick to suggest Dollar Point as the site. This drew a furious barrage of criticism from Nevada where residents of Virginia City had proposed Mt. Davidson for the site. The war of words dragged on until the honor was bestowed on Mt. Hamilton in Santa Clara County.

The shallows off Dollar Point southwest to Tahoe Park rest on a shelf of lava rock deposited by Mt. Pluto. This shelf is perforated with sunken valleys and ravines which are fascinating to observe from a boat when the lake is calm.

In 1970, the wooded acres on Dollar Point were in the throes of massive development. Trees were being cut, pipes being laid, and roads being bulldozed.

Pipe laying was a familiar scene everywhere on the North Shore owing to a provision in the Porter-Cologne Act which calls for the export of all sewage from the Tahoe Basin by January 1, 1972.

There's faint prospect the North Shore can meet this deadline. At last report, the authorities were still scratching their head, trying to decide where to export the treated effluent. If it is returned to the Truckee River, the communities of Reno and Sparks are liable to sue on the grounds of pollution. If the effluent is delivered elsewhere, the farmers who depend on the Truckee for irrigation seem certain to ask for an injunction.

Meanwhile, the treated effluent is being discharged on a 17-acre plot of National Forest near Tahoe City. This area, known as the Cinder Cone, is layered with highly porous rock.

A crisis came to light in the fall of 1970 when the utility districts asked permission of the Forest Service to increase the daily discharge from 1.25 million gallons to 2.8 million gallons and to extend the lease on the Cinder Cone to December 1975. The Forest Service refused on the grounds this might overtax the capacity of the Cinder Cone and pollute the Truckee.

Thereupon, the Tahoe City PUD proposed a moratorium on all new construction. This alarmed the developers and county officials. It was argued a moratorium would harm the tax base and make it all but impossible to finance the pipe laying necessary for the export system.

The Forest Service finally relented. It agreed to accept 2.8 million gallons daily provided semi-weekly bacteriology reports showed no contamination of the Truckee. But there was no agreement to extend the lease on the Cinder Cone beyond the regular cut-off date of December 1973.

So the crisis was postponed but by no means resolved. By the end of 1973, the discharge of effluent may well exceed 4 million gallons daily, while the export system may still be a year or two away from completion.

If no solution is found, summer residents face the prospect of having their cottages padlocked.

From Dollar Point, the highway drops almost to lake level at

Carnelian Bay, which was first known as Cornelian Bay. It was named for the semi-precious stones found on its shore by the Whitney Survey party in 1860. The earliest resort opened in 1871. This was Dr. Bourne's Hygienic Establishment, noted for its "hot and cold" mineral springs.

All the early settlers at Tahoe grew their own vegetables. In the rich alluvial soil bordering Carnelian Creek, carrots grew five inches thick.

On a lazy day in 1883, a party fishing on Carnelian Bay suddenly found its boat spinning in a whirlpool. One man lowered a sack tied to a rope over the side and it was pulled from his grasp into a hole on the lake bottom. This incident was reported in the Sacramento Union. Much later, the readers of the Virginia City newspaperman, Sam Davis, were treated to a fantastic yarn entitled, "The Mystery of the Savage Sump."

In substance, the story relates how a San Francisco stockbroker, William Meeker, discovered a hole on the floor of Carnelian Bay and used it to make a fortune.

As an experiment, Meeker dropped a log in the hole and found it a few days later in the sump of the Savage Mine at Virginia City. This led Meeker to believe that Tahoe was to blame for the mysterious flooding which forced many mines in the Comstock to close from time to time.

Working with his partner, Colonel Clair, in San Francisco, Meeker bought stock in the Savage Mine. Then he plugged the hole in Carnelian Bay. The flooding stopped, the miners resumed work, and the stock began to climb. When the price was right, Meeker wired Clair to sell short. Then he pulled the plug, allowing the mine to flood again. And so it went until, one eerie moonless night, Meeker was visited by his partner who struck him on the head and lowered him into the whirlpool. The enigmatic Colonel Clair departed from the scene of his crime, a

The Brockway Hotel and Hot Springs Resort in 1890. Boat in the foreground is the little steamer Wildwood of Brockway. *From the collection at the California State Library.*

multi-millionaire and the only man alive who knew the secret of Carnelian Bay.

Carnelian Bay has several resorts but "playland-at-the-beach" really begins next door at Agate Beach, named in 1860 by the surveyor, George Goddard.

Here we pass through Tahoe Vista, first known as Pine Grove Station when D. H. Wright established an inn and stable here in 1865. At this time, the Central Pacific had laid its track as far as Clipper Gap. From here, freight was forwarded in wagons to Donner Lake on the Dutch Flat Road which the railroad built to lure traffic away from the Great Bonanza Road.

From Donner Lake, a rough track ran by way of Martis Valley over a shoulder of Mt. Pluto to Agate Bay and thence along the shore to Incline on Crystal Bay. Out of Incline, there was a pack trail which climbed the Carson Range to Incline Summit and snaked down the east slope to historic Franktown in the Washoe Valley.

Pine Grove Station prospered until the railroad was completed to Reno. Then it became a depot for logs chuted down the slopes of Martis Peak. The smoking timbers would catapult into the lake where they were rafted and towed to Walter Hobart's mill on Crystal Bay.

Tahoe Vista was the name given a swank subdivision laid out on the site of Pine Grove Station about 1911. The developer's hopes of attracting the carriage trade were dashed when the buyer of the first lot proved to be Miss Cherry de St. Maurice of Sacramento, the proprietress of a highly successful bordello.

The Brockway Golf Course divides Tahoe Vista from King's Beach, the busy site of motels, resorts, trailer parks, gas stations, pizza parlors, burger drive-ins, real estate offices, and movie theatres, including one that features horror shows. Competition was so keen in 1970 that some motels advertised free use of a boat.

95

Steam launch Truckee *at Campbell's Hot Springs
(Brockway) in 1873. This boat operated on the lake
from 1870 until it was condemned as unseaworthy
in 1881. It was used to carry passengers and freight
and for towing logs. From the collection at the
California State Library.*

Legend has it that Joe King, who founded King's Beach in 1925, acquired the property in a poker game.

Between the golf course and King's Beach, the highway is joined by the Martis Valley Road which is California Route 267. This road was constructed in 1869 for the purpose of freighting cordwood to Truckee. One of the builders, the stage owner, William Campbell, bought frontage at the end of the road on which he built the celebrated Campbell's Hot Springs Hotel.

The name was changed when the hotel was purchased by Frank Brockway at the turn of the century. The Brockway Casino, built in 1917, was situated so the state line ran through the ballroom.

The site of Brockway lies just east of King's Beach where Nevada 28 bends and climbs to contour around Stateline Point. In 1970, the eighty-year-old hotel and all its furnishings were auctioned by the Brockway Development Company for the benefit of the North Lake Tahoe Historical Society and the Sacramento Symphony's Ford Foundation Fund Drive.

Among the items up for bid were hand-made Indian rugs, fine table linens, the hotel bar, an old post office, and eighty cottages. In this fashion, the last citadel of Victorian elegance vanished from the North Shore.

Squaw Valley is the largest of 16 ski areas in or near the Tahoe Basin.

X SQUAW VALLEY AND THE TRUCKEE RIVER

"With a friend and his two little sons, I have just returned from a week of bracing weathering around Lake Tahoe, in which we enjoyed glorious views of winter, fine rolling and sliding in the snow, swimming in the icy lake, and lusty reviving exercise on snow-shoes that kept our pulses dancing right merrily."—LAKE TAHOE IN WINTER by John Muir, 1878

On the southern edge of the Smoke Creek Desert, 33 miles northeast of Reno, is Pyramid Lake, a weird alkaline sink which is a remnant of the ancient Lahontan Sea. Pyramid runs about the same size as Tahoe; it contains trout and is surrounded by mountains. Otherwise, the two lakes have nothing in common except the fact they are linked by the beautiful Truckee River.

The Spanish for trout is "trucha." Allowing poetic license on the part of a frontiersman or Indian, this word might explain the origin of the name Truckee. But it's likely Truckee was the name of a person. Historians speculate he may have been the Indian who guided the Townsend-Murphy-Stevens party, or possibly a French trapper who accompanied the Bonneville-Walker expedition in the 1830's.

Fremont referred to the Truckee as the Salmon-Trout River and this name appears on maps published as late as 1858.

On its hundred mile descent to Pyramid Lake, the Truckee loses 2,460 feet in elevation. However, the drop-off is moderate on the first fourteen miles of the river from Tahoe City to the town of Truckee. Here, in a romantic forested canyon, is classic trout water, boulder-strewn and oxygenated by gentle riffles. Highway 89 closely follows the river here, affording access to several streamside camps of the Tahoe National Forest.

There are 16 chair lifts at Squaw Valley.
This one climbs Squaw Peak.

The old Tahoe-Truckee Toll Road was hardly better than a jeep trail but on its dusty, twisting grades such celebrities as Ulysses S. Grant and the actress, Lily Langtree, were treated to one of the most thrilling stage rides in the West. The excitement was heightened by the spectacle of huge logs careening down the canyonsides on slender wooden chutes. To span the road, the logs would catapult from a platform similar to a ski jump and fall in the river with a mighty splash. This so-called "free carry" practice was abandoned after a log failed to clear the right-of-way and killed a team of horses.

The present drive does not invite leisurely sightseeing owing to the speed of the traffic. The road was vastly improved during the 1950's in anticipation of the crush at the Squaw Valley Winter Olympics.

We leave Tahoe City in the shadow on Twin Crags. As the river bends north, the road is forced to the water's edge by Thunder Cliff.

From the Tahoe City "Y" junction, it's four miles to the mouth of Bear Creek. Here are several motor lodges and nearby is the Powder Bowl, a small winter sports area with strong appeal for family skiers.

We turn off on the paved road that runs up Bear Creek. It's a mile to Deer Park, the site of soda and mineral springs. A hotel was built here in 1888. It flourished despite the stern regime of Mrs. John B. Scott who imposed a 10:00 P.M. curfew on her guests and allowed no intoxicating spirits on the premises.

Such resorts were popular with Forty-Niners who had struck it rich but felt nostalgia for the harsh discipline of the trail.

A footpath leaves the vicinity of Deer Park for Five Lakes in the Granite Chief area.

A mile farther is Alpine Meadows, a large ski area with twelve lifts. There are several motels and a day lodge.

Back on Highway 89, we proceed 1½ miles, crossing to the

Squaw Valley had more than 800,000 visitors in 1970.

west bank of the Truckee before turning left on the spur to Squaw Valley. A spectacular cul-de-sac, the valley is half a mile wide and bound on three sides by peaks which crest to 2,600 feet above the meadows.

A small number of Forty-Niners crossed the Sierra crest by way of Squaw Valley on a rough emigrant trail known as Scott's Route. Block and tackle were required to hoist wagons up the slopes of Squaw Peak. A road of sorts was built by the county in 1852 but there was almost no traffic after 1856. One reason the route was not popular was because of the vast amount of snow that falls in Squaw Valley—about 450 inches a year.

In November of 1858, Richard W. Bucke and Ethan Allan Grosch, while en route to Sacramento, were stranded by a blizzard in Squaw Valley. Grosch was carrying maps, claims, and assays of silver ore which he and his brother, Hosea, had accumulated while prospecting the site of what became known a year later as the Comstock Lode. The documents and ore samples were lost when Grosch perished on the trail of exposure. Richard Bucke lost a leg and foot but survived to become a prominent physician in Canada.

Squaw Valley was homesteaded in 1862 by Ira A. Fish, who, with several partners, pioneered a large hay and dairy farm. It was this group who launched the schooner, "Iron Duke," at Tahoe. The valley's exports of milk, butter, and cheese declined after irrigation brought competition from the lowlands. There may have been skiing at Squaw Valley as early as the 1880's. But it was still a wild, lonely place when Wayne Poulsen, a champion skier at the University of Nevada, bought 1,800 acres here in 1944.

Poulsen retained 1,300 acres for subdivision. The rest was assigned to the Squaw Valley Development Company which Poulsen organized in partnership with Alex Cushing, a shrewd business head who eventually gained control of the firm.

Billed as the "world's largest cable car," the Squaw Valley Aerial Tram climbs to a restaurant 2,000 feet above Olympic Village.

It was Cushing who sparked the aggressive promotion to bring the 1960 winter Olympics to Squaw Valley. A total of 693 athletes from thirty countries participated. There were facilities for most every winter sport, except bobsledding. The U. S. fared poorly in skiing but won gold medals in hockey and figure skating. The overall winner by the unofficial point system was the Soviet Union.

More than a decade later, the Olympic Village remains intact as a highly popular State Recreation Area with 800,000 visitors a year. The indoor ice arena, which seats 8,000 spectators, serves as a public skating rink in winter and as a convention hall in summer. There are 29 lifts, including a cable lift billed as the "world's largest aerial tramway." It climbs to a restaurant perched 2,000 feet above the valley. Other facilities include tennis courts, a heated swimming pool, stables, shops, motels, inns, and a hotel with 320 rooms. Nearby is the family-oriented Papoose Ski Area.

While the concessionaires make a profit, the state pays out in excess of $200,000 a year to provide essential services. Critics say this amounts to a taxpayers' subsidy of private enterprise. The state cannot press for more favorable terms until the leases expire in 1988. So the Division of Parks and Recreation has been directed to sell the Olympics complex, but nobody seems to want the property because of the obligations that go with it. When the SRA was put up for auction in April of 1971, there was a single bid of $25,000 by John Stevenson, son of the late Adlai Stevenson. This offer could not be taken seriously in light of the millions both California and the federal government had poured into the development.

The concessionaires have their problems. In the winter of 1970, the aerial tramway stalled, stranding 121 passengers 300 feet above the ground. The following season, eight skiers were injured when a cable derailed on the Emigrant Lift. Shortly after

Average annual snowfall at Squaw Valley is 450 inches.

this incident, Alex Cushing's Swiss-born manager, Hans Burkhart, quit, charging the equipment was "junk." In his rebuttal, Cushing pointed out the lifts had borne two billion passengers in 21 years with only three mishaps and no fatalities.

As at Tahoe, there is smog, weekend traffic jams, and creeping urbanization which threatens the still unspoiled Squaw Valley Meadow. There are 400 living units in the subdivisions. Upwards to 7,500 skiers use the lifts on a holiday weekend. County planners have projected an eventual peak of 5,200 living units and as many as 20,000 skiers in a day. This estimate boggles the mind, allowing for the congestion which presently occurs on winter weekends. There's only one feasible route in and out of the valley unless a tunnel is blasted through the semi-circle of peaks.

At issue are the ski runs. These are beautiful in winter but when the snow melts, they emerge as ugly, treeless scars prone to damage by erosion. Alex Cushing wants to extend his maze of runs and lifts to Shirley Canyon where Squaw Creek rises. This move is bitterly opposed by valley residents who prefer the canyon as a natural area.

Just over Squaw Peak stretches the 39,000-acre Granite Chief back country. This is ruggedly beautiful region of high meadows, forested valleys, and granite promontories. It is laced with trails which approach several small lakes and some good trout streams.

In 1968, the Greater North Lake Tahoe Chamber of Commerce called on the Forest Service to cease building logging roads into the lovely Five Lakes Area that adjoins the south slope of Squaw Peak. The Forest Service was criticized for exploiting the region as a "cheap timber area." It was charged that logs were being cut here for export to Japan as pulp wood at the expense of the area's recreation potential.

The Forest Service responded with a proposal to restrict entry

Squaw Valley Meadow. Hay cut here in the 1860s was shipped to Lake Valley on the schooner Iron Duke.

*Squaw Valley's 29 lifts will accommodate 8,000 skiers
in a day.*

of motor vehicles into the northern half of the Granite Chief area. The southern half would be dedicated to "multiple use" which, in the patois of the Forest Service, usually means lumbering. The Sierra Club appealed this decision but was turned down on the grounds the south portion contained too much private land to be managed as wilderness.

A map available at ranger stations of the Tahoe National Forest shows the boundaries of the 20,400-acre roadless area which was established in April of 1970. The restriction on motor vehicles applies to snowmobiles as well as conventional cars. Considerable acreage in the attractive Five Lakes area was purchased by the non-profit Nature Conservancy for eventual transfer to the Forest Service.

A short way down canyon from the entrance to Squaw Valley, the highway spans the mouth of Squaw Creek. Across the river here was Knoxville, which grew from nothing to a town of 1,000 people in 1863. This population vanished the following year when assays of silver ore failed to prove out. The same fate befell nearby Claraville.

From Squaw Creek, it's 1½ miles to the Silver Creek USFS Campground which has 27 units, including eight suitable for trailers. A mile farther is Goose Meadows Camp, with nine units. It's another three miles to the Granite Flat Camp which has a few improved sites and numerous primitive clearings for tent campers.

The river off these camps is heavily stocked with pan-sized rainbow trout. These are fairly easy to catch, whereas the resident brown trout which range to 3-4 pounds pose a challenge for the most experienced angler.

The Truckee River off Highway 89 near Granite Flat.

*By winter the snow fans come from all over the West
to Squaw Valley for skiing.*

BIBLIOGRAPHY

Bowers, Nathan A. *Cone-Bearing Trees of the Pacific Coast*. Palo Alto: Pacific Books, 1961.

Brewer, William. *Up and Down California 1860-1864*. Berkeley and Los Angeles: University of California Press, 1949.

Bronson, William. *How to Kill a Golden State*. Garden City, New York: Doubleday & Company, 1968.

Clemens, Samuel L. (Mark Twain). *Roughing It*. Hartford: The American Publishing Co., 1899.

Cone, Mary. *Two Years in California*. Chicago: S. C. Griggs and Co., 1876.

Crofutt, George A. *New Overland Tourist and Pacific Coast Guide*. Omaha and Denver: The Overland Publishing Company, 1884.

Cross, Ralph Herbert. *The Early Inns of California 1844-1869*. San Francisco: Cross & Brandt, 1954.

Davis, William Morris. *"The Lakes of California,"* California Journal of Mines and Geology, Vol. 44, No. 2. San Francisco: Division of Mines, April 1948.

DeQuille, Dan (William Wright). *The Big Bonanza,* edition of 1876. Reprinted New York: Alfred A. Knopf, 1947.

Fatout, Paul. *Meadow Lake Gold Town*. Bloomington: Indiana University Press, 1969.

Farquhar, Francis P. *History of the Sierra Nevada*. Berkeley and Los Angeles: University of California Press, 1969.

Finck, Henry T. *The Pacific Coast Scenic Tour*. New York: Charles Scribner's Sons, 1890.

Frantz, Ted C. *"Food of Lake Trout in Lake Tahoe,"* Vol. 56, No. 1. Sacramento: California Fish and Game Quarterly, 1970.

Frantz, Ted C. *"Trout Catch and Angler Use at Lake Tahoe in 1962,"* Vol. 51, No. 3. Sacramento: California Fish and Game Quarterly, 1965.

Geiger and Bryarly. *Trail to California*. Edited by David Morris Potter. New Haven: Yale University Press, 1945.

113

Gudde, Erwin G. *California Place Names*. Berkeley and Los Angeles: University of California Press, 1965.

H. H. *Bits of Travel at Home*. Boston: Roberts Brothers, 1887.

Heller, Alfred E. *"Lake Tahoe: Time for Tough Federal Action."* Cry California, Winter 1965-66.

Hinds, Norman E. *Evolution of the California Landscape,* Bulletin 158. San Francisco: Division of Mines, 1952.

Hinkle, George and Bliss. *Sierra-Nevada Lakes*. New York: The Bobbs-Merrill Co., Inc., 1949.

Hoover, Rensch, and Abeloe. *Historic Spots in California*. Third edition, Stanford: Stanford University Press, 1966.

James, George Wharton. *The Lake of the Sky, Lake Tahoe*. Boston: L. C. Page & Co., 1915. Revised edition 1928.

LeConte, Joseph. *A Journey of Ramblings through the High Sierra of California*. Edition of 1875. Reprinted San Francisco: The Sierra Club, 1930.

Lee, Stone, Gale, and others. *Guidebook of the Western United States*. Washington, D. C.: U. S. Geological Survey, 1916.

Lewis, Oscar. *High Sierra Country*. New York: Duell, Sloan and Pearce. Boston, Toronto: Little Brown and Co., 1955.

Kroeber, A. L. *Handbook of the Indians of California*. Washington, D. C.: Smithsonian Institute, Bulletin 78, 1925.

Long, Love, and Merrill. *Alpine Heritage, 100 Years in Alpine County 1864-1964*. Markleeville: The Centennial Book Committtee, 1964.

Lowe, Don and Roberta. *100 Northern California Hiking Trails*. Portland, Oregon: The Touchstone Press, 1970.

Muir, John. *Lake Tahoe in Winter,* The Sierra Club Bulletin, Vol. IV, 1900-1901. San Francisco: The Sierra Club, 1950.

Schwenke and Winnett. *Sierra North*. Second edition, Berkeley: Wilderness Press, May 1971.

Scott, Edward B. *The Saga of Lake Tahoe*. Crystal Bay, Lake Tahoe, Nevada: Sierra-Tahoe Publishing Co., 1957.

Stewart, George R. *Donner Pass*. Menlo Park: Lane Books, 1959.

Stewart, George R. *The California Trail.* New York: McGraw-Hill Book Company, 1971.

Stewart, Patricia. *Touring TV's Mighty Ponderosa.* Nevada Highways and Parks, Summer 1971.

Storer and Usinger. *Sierra Nevada Natural History.* Berkeley and Los Angeles: University of California Press, 1963.

Taylor, Ron. *Subdividing the Wilderness,* The Sierra Club Bulletin. San Francisco: The Sierra Club, January 1971.

Tharratt, Bob. *An Exciting New Era,* Outdoor California. Sacramento: California Fish and Game Department, July-August 1970.

Toll, David. *Other Roads to California.* Nevada Highways and Parks, Fall 1969.

Wales, J. H. *Trout of California.* Sacramento: California Fish and Game, 1957.

Ware, Joseph. *The Emigrants' Guide to California.* Reprinted from the 1849 edition, Princeton: Princeton University Press, 1932.

Willden, Nye. *Lake Tahoe: "Something for Everyone."* Cavalier Magazine, January 1971.

Winnett and Denison. *The Tahoe-Yosemite Trail.* Berkeley: Wilderness Press, 1970.

Wood, Robert S. *Desolation Wilderness.* Berkeley: Wilderness Press, 1970.

Wood, Robert S. *Desolation Wilderness,* The Sierra Club Bulletin. San Francisco: The Sierra Club, March 1971.

Wyman, Walker D. *California Emigrant Letters.* New York: Bookman Associates, 1952.

————. *California Historical Landmarks.* California Division of Beaches and Parks.

————. *The Diaries of Peter Decker,* edited by Helen S. Giffen, 1849. Reprinted Georgetown, California: The Talisman Press, 1966.

————. *Gold Rush Country.* Menlo Park: Lane Publishing Company, 1957.

————. *Lake Valley's Past,* compiled by Lorene Greuner. South Lake Tahoe: Lake Tahoe Historical Society, 1971.

NEWSPAPERS:

Alpine Beacon (Markleeville)
Bridgeport Chronicle-Union
Nevada State Journal
Reno Evening Gazette
Sacramento Bee
San Francisco Chronicle
San Francisco Examiner
Sierra Sun (Truckee)
Tahoe City World
Tahoe Daily Tribune

INFORMATION SOURCES:

Alpine Chamber of Commerce, Markleeville, California 96120

Bureau of Land Management, Federal Office Building, 2800 Cottage Way, Room E-2841, Sacramento, California 95825

Department of Parks and Recreation, P. O. Box 2390, Sacramento, California 95811

El Dorado National Forest, 100 Forni Road, Placerville, California 95667

North Lake Tahoe Chamber of Commerce, Box 884, Tahoe City, California 95730

South Lake Tahoe Chamber of Commerce, P. O. Box 3418, South Lake Tahoe, California 95705

Stanislaus National Forest, 175 South Fairview Lane, Sonora, California 95370

Tahoe National Forest, Highway 49 and Coyote Street, Nevada City, California 95959

Toiyabe National Forest, Post Office Building, P. O. Box 1331, Reno, Nevada 89504

U. S. Bureau of Reclamation, Region 2, Sacramento, California, 95812

U. S. Corps of Engineers, 630 Sansome Street, San Francisco, California 94111.

Lake Tahoe Area Council, P. O. Box 3475, South Lake Tahoe, California 95705

INDEX

118

119

120